STUDENT RESOURCE GUIDE

for

THE LIFESPAN

Fifth Edition

by Guy Lefrançois

Thomas A. Tutko

Wadsworth Publishing Company

I(T)P® An International Thomson Publishing Company

Belmont • Albany • Bonn • Boston • Cincinnati • Detroit • London • Madrid • Melbourne
Mexico City • New York • Paris • San Francisco • Singapore • Tokyo • Toronto • Washington

CONTENTS

INTRODUCTION

You are about to embark on one of the most meaningful experiences of your college career. The reason this is true is because the material is so extremely personal.

This course will cover information that your family members have probably been discussing for years. You will become more in tune with your family values, how they were, are, could have been and might be.

This course will provide you with the opportunity to become the family lifespan expert answering questions for any age on all major topics.

Each chapter has facts and information that you have either lived, are living or will live. It will help you assess major decisions you will make in your life whether it be higher education and finances, marriage and having a family or work decisions and retirement.

You will have the benefit of the knowledge and experiences accrued by others in every critical aspect of life. As a result of this course you will have the opportunity to plan your future far better than you might have otherwise. The information can help you construct a life not only avoiding pitfalls but creating the journey of your dreams.

Since this course is so personal, so meaningful it deserves a different format for studying. This Student Resource Guide is a departure from the traditional approach and is based on the premise that for material to be "truly" learned, it involves three steps. The first step is to read and understand, the second to study and comprehend and the third phase is to experience.

Each chapter in the Student Resource Guide is divided into three sections. A further breakdown is described below.

I.   Reading and Understanding

Many students feel that if they read the material they automatically understand it. To test this assumption an outline is provided for each chapter. Once you have completed the chapter go through the outline and try to recall as much as you can for each segment in the outline. Material read is not always understood. An added challenge to understanding the reading is to test yourself by referring to the study terms at the end of each chapter. All courses in college have their own language. Each chapter has its unique language. Test yourself by defining each key term. If you can define the terms and explain the outline you have made the first major step in "truly" learning the material.

II.   Studying and Comprehending

This Student Resource Guide makes a major departure from traditional study guides on how to study the contents of each chapter. Two concepts, flashcards and scrambles are introduced, each with a different intent. Although your exams may be the traditional i.e., multiple choice, true-false, matching, etc. by using the flashcards and scrambles you will be well prepared for any sort of exam.

A. Flashcards

The purpose of flashcards is to provide you with a proactive not a passive approach to studying. The cards are arranged in the same reading order as the text. Each flashcard represents a different type of potential question i.e., definition, explanation, clarification, enumeration, etc.

The way to use the flashcard is as follows. As you read the material and run across terms on the flashcards put the appropriate information on the back of the card. Make up a multiple-choice question, true-false question, etc. similar to the one you will have in the exam for your class. Once you have completed the chapter and have all of the flashcards filled, cut them out and form a deck of cards for that chapter. Notice there are more terms in these cards than appearing at the end of the chapter. In time you will learn to develop flashcards more fitting to the class and the material. For the time being these cards should be more than adequate to prepare for a test. Mix up the cards and go through them. Because you have written the answer on the back it will be easier to remember and thus easier to recall come test time.

You won't be able to remember them all so put the ones you know in one pile and the ones you will need to study in another pile. These two piles already give you an idea of how much you know and how much you need to study. You may even want to tabulate the percentage of cards you know giving you some idea of what you might get on that chapter in an exam. Ultimately when all the cards are in the "I know" pile you are ready for the exam. It is a different way to approach exam material rather than just reading and hope it sticks in your head.

Notice that this is a recall type of quiz, i.e., you have to recall all of the information. The next type of studying -- using scrambles is a recognition type of exam.

B. Scrambles

Scrambles present a summary of materials and you must recognize where it fits. This is not true of every scramble. Some require you to recall the material. These however are less frequent than the recognition types. The purpose of a scramble is to recognize and organize the material appropriately.

In addition, a scramble usually involves a large amount of material and requires you to separate it not only logically but in an organized fashion.

Scrambles are intended to be fun in addition to providing you with information. They are of two types. The first are those scrambles already appearing in the form of table or a figure in the book. The second type are those scrambles devised from the reading material. Differences in the two types will become apparent to you.

Each scramble is worth a certain number of points that you can tabulate after it is completed. The percentage you get represents (as with the flashcards) how much of the material in the chapter you have learned. At the end of all the scrambles is a scramble summary where you can get an overall chapter percentage letting you know how well prepared you are for the exam.

NOTE: Flashcards are more thorough and detailed than scrambles and some material lends itself more readily to one form of studying than another. Although most material can be covered through these two approaches they are not totally complete. You may wish to develop your own flashcards or scrambles and exchange them with your friends making your studying more complete.

III.   Experiencing

Truly learning the material goes beyond reading-understanding and studying-comprehending. This dimension is called experiencing. Once you experience the material it takes on a whole new meaning. To this end exercises for the main points have been created.

You will notice at the end of each chapter the author summarizes this through main points. To make certain these truly personal exercises have been developed to challenge how fluent you are with the material. The purpose of the exercises are twofold. The first is to have you explore how well you know the material by applying it. Secondly the main points are commonly the kinds of questions you, your family and friends have asked, not only of yourselves but of each other. They have been things we have all wondered about but for which we did not always know the answers.

Learning the material goes beyond scores made on tests or answers on a questionnaire. Knowledge from the Lifespan course involves everyday living, everyday puzzles—questions and answers.

These exercises have been arranged to test how fluent you are with the material; how well you can explain to someone what you have learned.

Your instructor may use these in a number of different ways. You may be required to role play them in class, hand in as a project, work with in a small group to come to decisions, discuss in front of others, produce a mini lecture, etc. They have been arranged in such a way that you may find them useful in everyday interaction, to answer friends questions (or some of your own).

At times they may seem too personal. Feel free to avoid them (but not without thinking why they leave you so uptight.)

The final purpose of the exercise is to give you an opportunity to grow personally in two ways. One is to discuss these highly personal things with others, including friends and loved ones. The other is self exploration--to explore where you have been, where you are and how you got that way. The final step is to explore where you want to go and why. The purpose of the Student Resource Guide is to help you on this journey.

I. Reading and Understanding

Studying Human Development
Chapter I

This Text.
Lifespan
Developmental Psychology
--Psychology
--Developmental Psychology
--Lifespan Developmental Psychology
      The Lifespan Perspective
            Development Is Continuous
            Maturity Is Relative
            Development Occurs in Context
            --ecology
            Developmental Influences are Bidirectional
            --bidirectionality
Some Definition In Development
--Growth
--Motivation
--Learning
--Development (growth-maturation-learning)
Historical Snapshots
      Snapshot 1: Child Rearing, Medieval Europe
      Snapshot 2: Begging in l8th-Century Europe
      Snapshot 3: Child, Abandonment, 18th Century
      Snapshot 4: Child Labor in the l9th Century
      Snapshot 5: The Developing World Today
      Snapshot 6: The Industrialized World
Children's Rights
      Historical Lack of Rights
      --baby tossing
      Children's Rights Today
Studying Human Development
      Early Pioneers
            Locke
            --tabula rasa
            Rousseau
      Later Pioneers
            Hall
            --Ontogeny
            Watson
Recurring Questions
--nature-nurture controversy
--stages
Methods of Studying the Lifespan
--experimental
--longitudinal
--cross-sectional
      Observation
            Naturalistic Observation
            --naturalistic
            --diary descriptions
            --specimen descriptions
            --event sampling
            --time sampling
            Nonnaturalistic Observation

II. Learning and Comprehending

Scrambles
Chapter 1

Scramble 1

In appropriate time sequence match the correct historical period with the type of treatment rendered.

Historical Period	Treatment of Children	Point
_____	_____	_____
_____	_____	_____
_____	_____	_____
_____	_____	_____
_____	_____	_____
_____	_____	_____

Your Total Points: _____
Total Possible Points: 12
% _____

1. Child labor continues to flourish beginnings of important medical and educational changes.
2. Middle Ages
3. Poverty and emotional indifference lead to widespread abandonment of infants, very high infant mortality rates.
4. Renaissance
5. Child-centered, especially in the industrialized world, concern with the rights and plights of children. But there are still many instances of abuse starvation exploitation and unnecessary mortality.
6. l9th Century
7. 18th Century
8. Ambivalent attitude toward children
9. Antiquity
10. Industrialization contributes to widespread use of children as manual laborers to factories, mines, fields, shops
11. Little evidence of strong parental attachment, occasional infanticide socially acceptable
12. 20th Century

Scramble 2.   **In the appropriate time sequence match the pioneer with the appropriate philosophical position.**

<u>Pioneer</u>	<u>Philosophical Position</u>	<u>Points</u>
_____	_____	_____
_____	_____	_____
_____	_____	_____
_____	_____	_____

Your Total Points: _____
Total Possible Points: 12
% = _____

1.   Ontogeny recapitulates phylogeny
2.   Rousseau
3.   experimental learning theory based approach
4.   Watson
5.   Tabula rasa
6.   Locke
7.   "noble savage"
8.   Hall

Scramble 3: **Match the Method, Description and Main Uses of the following Naturalistic Observations in Developmental Research**

Method	Description	Main Use	Points:
_____	_____	_____	_____
_____	_____	_____	_____
_____	_____	_____	_____
_____	_____	_____	_____

Your Total Points: _____
Total Possible Points: 12
% = _____

1. Detailed description of sequences of behavior, detailing all aspects of behavior.
2. Specific behaviors (events) are recorded during the observational period and other behaviors are ignored.
3. Time sampling.
4. Understanding the nature and frequency of specific behaviors (events).
5. Fairly regular (often daily or weekly) descriptions of important events and changes.
6. Event sampling
7. Specimen description.
8. Detecting and understanding major changes and developmental sequences.
9. Investigator records what prisoner is doing during 30-second spans, once every 30 minutes
10. Detecting and assessing changes in specific behaviors over time.
11. Diary description.
12. Investigator notes each time child bangs her head on the wall.
13. Studying individual children in depth, not restricted to only one or two predetermined characteristics.
14. Investigator videotapes sequences of woman's behavior for later analysis.
15. Behaviors are recorded intermittently during short but regular periods of time.
16. Investigator keeps detailed sequential record of child's speech.

Scramble Summary

Scramble 1	**Historical Period and Treatment**	_____	**12**
Scramble 2	**Pioneers Philosophical Position**	_____	**8**
Scramble 3	**Naturalistic Observations**	_____	**1**

Your Total Scores _____
Total Possible Score 32
% = _____

III.   **Experiencing**

Main Points and Exercises

Exercises
Chapter 1

Lifespan Developmental Psychology

1.   The contemporary lifespan view of development recognizes that change continues throughout the lifespan, that maturity is a relative and changing state, that it is important to consider the context (*ecology*) of human development, and that developmental influences are bidirectional.

Exercise 1:   You are discussing the courses you are taking with a friend. When you tell them you are taking "Lifespan Developmental Psychology" they ask "What's that?" Briefly describe the lifespan perspective using the 4 concepts that marks the lifespan approach as different (continuous, maturity, context, bidirectional). You may want to use mnemonic cues to assist you. (CMCB).

1b.   Some Definitions In Development:

Historical Snapshots

2.   There is evidence that in medieval times the concept of childhood did not exist as we know it, that parent-child attachment was indifferent, and that infant mortality was very high. Through the l8th and l9th centuries, child labor flourished, and child-rearing practices were often harsh and cruel by current North American standards. The 20th century brought increasing concern with the social, physical, and intellectual welfare of children, especially in the industrialized world.

Exercise 2:   *Scenario*. You re a parent with several children. You meet a friend and they ask you--"How are the kids." Write a single sentence which would best reflect the attitude of the times:

Medieval Europe:

l8th Century:

l9th Century:

6

Developing World Today:

Children's Rights

3.   The recognition of children's rights--a relatively recent international development--describes rights of protection and to growth-fostering conditions (rather than the more adult rights of choice).

Scenario: You are a parent who feels your child is not being given adequate protection at school. Prepare a paragraph on Children Rights that you would use in presenting your case to the school board. Base it on any issue you feel important. (-12)

Studying Human Development

4.   Among early pioneers in the scientific study of human development were John Locke (*tabula rasa)* and Jean-Jacques Rousseau ("noble savage"). Later pioneers included Charles Darwin (child biography and evolution), G. Stanley Hall ("ontogeny recapitulates phylogeny"), and John B. Watson (we become what we are a function of our experiences).

Exercise 4:   Select any of the early pioneers --Locke, Rousseau, Hall or Watson and point out why you feel the position best represents children.

Methods of Studying the Lifespan

5.   Observation is the basis of all science. Naturalistic observation occurs when individuals are observed without interference (diary descriptions, specimen descriptions, event sampling, and time sampling). Nonnaturalistic observations may be clinical (using questionnaires or interviews, or experimental (deliberately manipulating the environment). Experiments are useful for investigating cause-and-effect relationships, as are correlational studies (studies of relationships) that provide useful information about cause-and-effect relationships *but cannot prove causation.*

Exercise 5a: List a particular behavior you would like to observe in a child. Point out which of the 4 techniques you would use and how you would do it.

Exercise 5b:　You are submitting a grant proposal for funding of a particular experiment. List below all of the details of your experiment description of the experiment:

Hypothesis:

Independent Variable:

Dependent Variable:

Anticipated Results

Exercise 5c:　You are submitting a grant proposal for funding a particular correlational study. List below the details of your study. What variables are you going to correlate and what are the anticipated results?

6.　　Longitudinal studies examine the same individuals at different periods in their lives; cross-sectional studies compare different individuals at the same time. Longitudinal studies may be more costly and time-consuming and may suffer from problems relating to subject (9r experimenter) mortality and the eventual obsolescence of experimental methods and instruments. Cross-sectional studies are useful for comparing groups of different ages at one time but provide little information about intra-individual changes.

Exercise 6:　Select an area of research that you would like to pursue using the longitudinal study. Now describe how you would hope to find the same results using the cross sectional approach?

7.　　A cohort is a group of individuals born during a single timespan and often subject to a variety of unique influences that might account for important differences between them and members of other cohorts. Attempts to reduce the confounding of age and cohort in developmental research have led to *sequential* research designs--so called because they involve the selection of a sequence of samples. A time-lag study is a sequential design in which different cohorts are compared at different times with age held constant.

Exercise 7a: List 5 values important to your grandparents.

1.

2.

3.

4.

5.

List 5 values important to your parents.

1.

2

3

4

5

List 5 values important to you.

1.

2.

3.

4.

5.

7b.   What values have remained consistent with the family? What values have markedly changed within the family? What do you think of your grandparents values? Your parents values? What do they think of yours?

7c.   To make the cohort values more specific do the same exercise centering values around:

--jobs

--money

--marriage

--children

--divorce

Criteria for Evaluating Lifespan Research

8.   The validity and reliability of research results are subject to the influences of sample size and representativeness, ecological and cross-cultural validity, subject memory and honesty, experimenter and subject biases, and cohort-related experiences. There are also ethical issues to be considered in doing lifespan research.

Exercise 8:   Harvey has found a new drug he feels will help reduce fear and anxiety to patients who have dental work. He is afraid, however, that if he does an experiment to prove it works, the dentist will be less anxious and that may confuse the research. Describe to him how he can use a "double-blind experiment to get around the problem.

The Mythical Average

9.   The average individual is a conceptually useful invention but does not exist. Nor does the average context. Global environmental change presents a serious challenge for developmental psychologists--and for all humans.

Exercise 9:   List 3 environmental changes that are taking place in your area that has long range manifestation for your people of tomorrow.

I.   Reading and Understanding

Theories of Lifespan Development
Chapter 2

This Chapter
--nominal fallacy
Psychological Theories
       --theory
       --naive theories
       --commonsense theories
Purposes of Theories
Evaluating Theories
       Characteristics of Good Theories
       --heuristic
Models in Lifespan Development
       Machine-Organism Models
       --organismic model
       --mechanistic model
              --active
              --reactive
A Contextual Model
       --contextual (or ecological) model
       --Bronfenbrenner's ecological systems theory
       --Vygotsky's social-cognitive theory
A Psychoanalytic Approach: Freud
       --Psychoanalytic theory
              --Freudian slips
Basic Freudian idea
       --Sexuality
              --libido
Three Levels of Personality
       Id
       --reflexes
       --psychic energy
       Ego
       --reality
       Superego
       --conscience
       --identifying
Freud's Psychosexual Stages
       --psychosexual
       The Oral Period
       --oral stage
       The Anal Period
       --anal stage
       The Phallic Stage
       --phallic
       --Oedipus complex
       --Electra complex
       Sexual Latency
       --latency
       --identification
       Genital Stage
       Freud in Review
       --unconscious

Humanistic Approaches
        --humanist
        --phenomenology
        Maslow's Humanistic Theory
        --basic needs
        --metaneeds
        --self-actualization
        --deficiency needs
        Maslow's hierarchy of needs
        Self-Actualization
        Humanism in Review

Scrambles
Chapter 2

Scramble 1:   **List the descriptive terms for each of the**
                                three basic models in Developmental Psychology.

	Organismic	Mechanistic	Contextual	Points
Metaphor	_____	_____	_____	____
Perception of Person	_____	_____	_____	____
Developmental Process			_____	____
Theories	_____	_____	_____	____
Emphasis	_____	_____	_____	____
Theorists	_____	_____	_____	____

Your Total Points   _____
Total Possible Points   18
% =   _____

1.   Attention to similarities; recognition of context-related differences
2.   Theories emphasizing the continuity of development
3.   Tends toward final adult stage, describable in terms of adult thought structures (logical characteristics of adult thought)
4.   Attention to individual differences
5.   A biological organism
6.   A plastic--strong, resilient, but responsive
7.   Attention to similarities
8.   Theories emphasizing the interaction of age, historical variables, important life events culture, and other aspects of context.
9.   Described in terms of learning and problem solving; no clearly described end goal
10. Sees individual as reactive, responsive to environment
11   Sees individual as active, self-directed
12. Urle Bronfenbrenner; Richard M. Lemer, K. Warner Schale, Gisela Labouvie-Viet, M. Bassaches, also contemporary behaviorists
13. A machine
14. Age-related stage theories emphasizing similarities of thought of each level
15. Involves universal principles influenced by the individual's specific social historical, and personal context
16. Jean Piaget, Sigmund Freud
17. Early behaviorism
18. Sees individual as active and reactive

Scramble 2:   Match the descriptive term with Freud's Levels of Personality

Level of Personality	Descriptive Term	Points
_____	_____	_____
_____	_____	_____
_____	_____	_____
	Your Total Points	_____
	Total Possible Points	6
	% =	_____

1.   Rational, intellectual level
2.   Conscience
3.   Ego
4.   Psychic energy
5.   Superego
6.   Id

Scramble 3: **Match Freud's Stages of Psychosexual Development with appropriate ages and characteristics.**

<u>Stage</u>	<u>Approximate Ages</u>	<u>Characteristics</u>	<u>Points</u>
_____	_____	_____	_____
_____	_____	_____	_____
_____	_____	_____	_____
_____	_____	_____	_____
_____	_____	_____	_____

Your Total Points   _____
Total Possible Points: l5
% =   _____

1. Sources of sexual gratification include expelling feces and urination, as well as retaining feces.
2. Oral
3. 2-3 to 6 years
4. 0 to l8 months
5. Sources of pleasure include sucking, biting, swallowing, playing with lips.
   Preoccupation with immediate gratification of impulses
   Id is dominant
6. Latency
7. Anal
8. Concern with adult modes of sexual pleasure, barring fixations of regressions
9. 6 to 11 years
10. Source of sexual pleasure involves manipulating genitals.
    Period of Oedipus or Electra complex
    Id, ego, and superego
11. l8 months to 2-3 years
12. Phallic
13. 11 and older
14. Loss of interest in sexual gratification
    Identification with like-sexed parent
    id, ego, and superego
15. Genital

Scramble 4:   **Match the Defense Mechanism with appropriate definition.**

Defense Mechanism	Description	Points
_____	_____	_____
_____	_____	_____
_____	_____	_____
_____	_____	_____
_____	_____	_____
_____	_____	_____

Your Total Points   _____
Total Possible Points   6
% =   _____

Defense Mechanism	Description
1. Behavior is stripped of its emotional meaning	A mercenary who fears his enjoyment of his work is unhealthy convinces himself he is moved by duty and not by love of killing
2. Undesirable emotions are directed toward a different object	A man who is angry at his wife kicks his dog
3. People attribute their own undesirable feelings or inclinations to others	A man who is extremely jealous of a competitor believes it is the competitor who is jealous of him
4. Unpleasant experiences are stored deep remembers in the subconscious mind and become inaccessible to waking memory	A child is sexually abused remembers nothing of the experience
5. Reality is distorted to make it conform to the individual's wishes	A heavy smoker is unable to give up the habit and decides that there is no substantial evidence linking nicotine with human diseases
6. Behavior is the opposite of the individual's actual feelings	A woman loves an unobtainable man and behaves as though she dislikes him

Scramble 5   **In the correct chronological sequence match Erickson's Psychosocial Stages with the Principal Developmental Task.**

Erickson's Psychosocial Stage   **Principle Developmental Task   Points**

_____   _____   _____

_____   _____   _____

_____   _____   _____

_____   _____   _____

_____   _____   _____

_____   _____   _____

_____   _____   _____

_____   _____   _____

Your Total Points   _____
Total Possible Points   16
% =   _____

1.   Intimacy vs. isolation
2.   Developing sufficient trust in the world to explore it
3.   Trust vs. mistrust
4.   Assuming responsible adult roles in the community, contributing being worthwhile
5.   Industry vs. inferiority
6.   Developing feeling of control over behavior, realizing that intentions can be acted out
7.   Integrity vs despair
8.   Developing a sense of self through identification with parents and a sense of responsibility for own actions
9.   Autonomy vs. shame and doubt
10. Ego (self) selecting among various potential selves
11. Identity vs. identity diffusion
12. Developing a sense of self-worth through interaction with news
13. Generativity vs. self-absorption
14. Facing death, overcoming potential despair; coming to terms with the meaningfulness of life
15. Initiative vs. guilt
16. Developing close relationships with others, achieving the intimacy required for marriage

Scramble 6:   List four developmental tasks outlined by Havighurst for each period

Period	Developmental Tasks	Points
Infancy and early childhood (birth through preschool period)	_____	----------
	_____	----------
	_____	----------
	_____	----------
Middle childhood (the elementary school period)	_____	----------
	_____	----------
	_____	----------
	_____	----------
Adolescence	_____	----------
	_____	----------
	_____	----------
	_____	----------
Young adulthood	_____	----------
	_____	----------
	_____	----------
	_____	----------
Middle adulthood	_____	----------
	_____	----------
	_____	----------
	_____	----------
Old Age	_____	----------
	_____	----------
	_____	----------
	_____	----------

Old age _____ ----------

_____ ----------

_____ ----------

_____ ----------

Your Total Points _____

Total Possible Points 24

% = _____

1. Counting and selecting a male
   Learning to live happily with partner
2. Adjusting to physical changes
   Adjusting to retirement and to changes in income
3. Achieving physiological rhythms in sleeping and eating
   Learning to take solid foods
4. Developing conceptual and problem-solving skills
   Achieving mature relationships with male and female peers
5. Learning skills necessary for physical games
   Building a positive self-concept
6. Assisting children in transition from home to world
   Developing adult leisure activities
7. Beginning to relate emotionally to parents and siblings
   Learning to talk
   Learning to control elimination body wastes
8. Establishing satisfactory living arrangements
   learning to live with spouse in retirement
   Adjusting death of spouse
9. Relating to spouse as a person
   Reaching adult social and civic responsibility
10. Assuming home management responsibilities
    Beginning career or occupation
11. Becoming personally independent; weakening family ties
    Developing basic reading, writing, and arithmetic skills
12. Preparing for an economically viable career
    Achieving emotional independence from parents
13. Assuming appropriate civic responsibilities
    Establishing a social network
14 Forming affiliations with aging peers
15. Developing an ethical system to guide behavior
    Striving toward socially responsible behavior
    Accepting the changing physique and using the body effectively
16. Developing an understanding of the self and the world
17. Learning to walk
    Learning to distinguish right from wrong
18. Maintaining satisfactory career performance
    Adjusting to physiological changes of middle age
19. Learning sex differences and sexual modesty
20. Adopting an appropriate masculine or feminine role
    Learning to get along with peers
    Developing values, a sense of morality, a conscience
21. Preparing for marriage and family life
22. Starting a family and assuming parent role
    Rearing children
23 Adjusting to aging parents
24. Adopting flexible social roles

Scramble 7:   **In chronological order match Piaget's Stages of Cognitive Development appropriate age and a major characteristic of that stage.**

Stage	Appropriate Age	Characteristic	Points
_____	_____	_____	___
_____	_____	_____	___
_____	_____	_____	___
_____	_____	_____	___

Your Total Points   _____
Total Possible Points   12
% =   _____

__Although other characteristics are possible only one is listed for this exercise.__

1. 7 to 11-12 years
2. Preoperational
3. Intelligence in action
   World of the here and how
   No language, no thought, no notion of objective reality at a beginning of stage
4. Concrete operations
5. Egocentric thought
   Reason dominated by perception
   Intuitive rather than logical solutions
   Inability to conserve
6. Formal operations
7. Ability to conserve
   Logic of classes and relations
   Understanding of numbers
   Thinking bound to concrete
   Development of reversibility in thought
8. 2 to 7 years
9. 0 to 2 years
10. 11-12 to l4-l5 years
11. Sensorimotor
12. Propositional thinking
    Ability to deal with the hypothetical
    Development of strong idealism

Scramble 8:   **Using Vygotsky's description of the Role of Language, list in chronological order stage with the function.**

Stage	Appropriate Age	Characteristic	Points
_____	_____	_____	_____
_____	_____	_____	_____
_____	_____	_____	_____
_____	_____	_____	_____

Your Total Points   _____
Total Possible Points   6
% =   _____

1. Bridge between external and inner speech; serves to control own behavior but spoken out loud
2. Social (external) speech (to age 3)
3. Self-talk; makes possible the direction of our thinking and our behavior; involved in all higher mental functioning
4. Egocentric speech (3 to 7)
5. Controls the behavior of others, expresses simple thoughts and emotions
6. Inner speech (7 onward)

Scramble 9:   **Match the Levels of Context to the type of interaction Bronfenbrenner's Ecological Systems.**

Level	Types of Interaction	Points
_____	_____	_____
_____	_____	_____
_____	_____	_____
_____	_____	_____

Your Total Points   _____
Total Possible Points   8
% =   _____

1. Relationships between two or more microsystems
2. Macrosystem
3. Child in immediate, face-to-face interaction
4. Exosystem
5. The totality of all other systems, evident in the beliefs, the options, the lifestyles, the values, the mores of a culture or subculture
6. Microsystem
7. Linkages and relationships between two or more settings, one of which does not include the child
8. Mesosystem

Scramble 10:   **Match the approach with the Theorist, Major Assumptions and the Key Terms.**

Approach	Theorist(s)	Major Assumptions	Key Terms	Points
Biological	_____	_____	_____	_____
Social-Cognitive	_____	_____	_____	_____
Descriptive	_____	_____	_____	_____
Psychoanalytic	_____	_____	_____	_____
Behavioristic	_____	_____	_____	_____
Cognitive	_____	_____	_____	_____
Ecological Systems	_____	_____	_____	_____
Humanistic	_____	_____	_____	_____

Your Total Points	_____
Total Possible Points	27
% =	_____

1. Bowlby, Wilson
2. Development consists of a series of culturally imposed tasks (competencies) imposed on the individual at different stages of the life cycle
3. Id, ego, superego, psychosexual fibration, regression
4. Observational learning leads to developmental change, our ability to symbolize and to anticipate the consequences of our behavior is fundamental as are our estimates of our self-efficacy
5. Self, positive growth, metaneeds, basic needs, self-actualization
6. Bandura
7. Child progresses through developmental stages by resolving conflicts that arise from a need to adapt to the sociocultural environment
8. Competence, social environment, developmental tasks, psychosocial
9. Social behaviors have a biological basis understandable in evolutionary terms. The formation of attachment bonds is one example
10. Maslow, Rogers
11. The ecology of development is the study of accommodations between a person and the environment (culture) taking the changing characteristics of each into account
12. Reinforcement, punishment, stimuli, responses
13. Changes in behavior are a function of reinforcement and punishment
14. Watson, Skinner
15. Individual is motivated by instinctual urges that are primarily sexual and aggressive
16. Stages, assimilation, accommodation, adaptation, schema
17. Havighurst
18. Imitation, modeling, eliciting, inhibiting-disinhibiting, self-efficacy
19. Erikson
20. Attachment bonds, biological fitness, survival value, altruistic genes, sensitive period
21. All individuals are unique but strive toward the fullest development of their potential
22. Piaget
23. Developmental tasks, social requirements, social adaptation, maturity
24. Child develops cognitive skills through active interaction with the environment
25. Vygotsky, Bronfenbrenner
26. Freud
27. Culture, language, open systems, ecology, microsystem, mesosystem, exosystem, macrosystem

Scramble Summary

		Your Score	Total Points
Scramble 1	Three Basic Models in Developmental Psychology	_____	18
Scramble 2	Freud-'s Levels of Personality	_____	6
Scramble 3	Freud's Stages of Psychosexual Development	_____	15
Scramble 4	Defense Mechanisms	_____	6
Scramble 5	Erickson's Psychosocial Stages	_____	14
Scramble 6	Havighurst's Developmental Tasks	_____	24
Scramble 7	Piaget's Theory	_____	12
Scramble 8	Vygotsky's Description of the Role of Language	_____	6
Scramble 9	Bronfenbrenner's Ecological Systems Theory	_____	8
Scramble 10	Approaches to Developmental Theory	_____	27

Your Total Scores _____
Total Possible Score 136
% = _____

III.   **Experiencing**

Main Points and Exercises

Exercises
Chapter 2

Psychological Theories

1.   A theory is a collection of statements intended to organize and explain important observations. Theories are best evaluated in terms of usefulness rather than truthfulness,. They should reflect "facts," be understandable, and be useful for predicting events as well as for explaining the past.

Exercise I.   Everyone has developed their own theories about something. Here is your chance to develop a theory and put it on paper. You may select one of the topics listed below or select one of your own. When you have finished writing your theory, check your observations with the characteristic of a good theory listed on p.5. Where have you met the criterion? Where have you fallen short?

Ideas:

1.   Why children exaggerate (fib, tell lies, etc.)
2.   Why parents abuse their children?
3.   Why some children become bullies?
4.   Why students cheat on exams?
5.   Why most college students are shy.

Models in Lifespan Development

2.   Models are metaphors that underlie theories. The organismic model describes people as active, functioning biological organisms; the mechanistic view stresses the reactive, machinelike of human functioning; the contextual model emphasized the influence of historical variables, life events, and other aspects of context.

Exercise 2.   If you were in a debate what would be your defense of each lifespan developmental **model?** Give a brief sentence to each listed below:

Organismic Model

Mechanistic Model

Contextual Model

A Psychoanalytic Approach: Freud

3.   Freud's theory is based on the assumption that among the most important causes of behavior are deep-seated, unconscious forces. The newborn child is all *libido* (instinctual urges), termed *id*, concerned solely with the gratification of primarily sexual urges. Conflict between the id and reality develops the *ego*, which tries to satisfy id urges within the constraints of reality. The *superego* (conscience) forms later and represents social and cultural taboos. Development involves progression through five stages (oral, anal, phallic, latency, and genital), each differentiated from the others primarily by the areas of the child's body that are the principal sources of sexual gratification at that time.

Exercise 3a.   List 3 adult behaviors that reflect Freud's level of personality.

Id   1

                2

                3

Ego   1

                2

                3

Superego   1

                2

                3

Exercise 4a: List 3 adult behaviors that reflect the following psychosexual stages of
development

Oral   1

                2

                3

Anal   1

                2

                3

Phallic   1

                2

                3

Sexual
Latency   1

                2

                3

Genital   1

                2

                3

A Psychosocial Approach: Erikson

4.   According to Erikson's *psychosocial* theory of development, the individual progresses through a series of stages characterized by basic conflicts, the resolution of which results in the appearance of new capabilities and attitudes; trust versus mistrust, autonomy versus shame and doubt, initiative versus guilt, industry versus inferiority, identity versus identity diffusion, intimacy versus isolation, generativity versus self-absorption, and integrity versus despair.

Exercise 4:   Listed below are Erickson's 8 Psychosexual Stages of Development along the Important Influences for Positive Development Outcome. Beside each influence is a rating scale from I to 5. Mark each influence based on your personal experience with I meaning very little positive influence, 3 meaning somewhat and 5 meaning a great deal.

Erickson's Scale

Psychosocial Stages	Important Influences for Positive Developmental Very Little		Somewhat		A Great Deal
Trust vs. Mistrust	Mother: warm, loving imitation	1	2	3	4	5
Autonomy vs. Shame and Doubt	Supportive parents, imitation	1	2	3	4	5
Initiative vs. Guilt	Supportive parents, identification	1	2	3	4	5
Industry vs. Inferiority	Schools, teachers, learning and education, encouragement	1	2	3	4	5
Identity vs. Identity Diffusion	Peers and role models, social pressure	1	2	3	4	5
Intimacy vs. Isolation	Spouse colleagues, partners, society	1	2	3	4	5
Generativity vs. Self-absorption	Spouse, children, friends, colleagues, community	1	2	3	4	5
Integrity vs. Despair	Friends, relatives, children, spouse, community and religious support	1	2	3	4	5

Based on these results write a very brief paragraph describing your resolution of Erickson's Psychosocial Stages.

Havighurst's Developmental Tasks

5.   Havighurst describes development in terms of a series of requirements that are placed on individuals by their society. These provide a rough index of developmental maturity.

Exercise 5.   Listed below are Havighurst's Developmental Tasks along with the age periods in which they are to occur for the first four periods of life. Make a checklist for each period. For the infancy stage ask your parents about the recollection of you at this stage. For the middle childhood, adolescent and your adulthood periods, try to recall as many as possible and your reaction to them. For middle adulthood and old age, make a checklist for your parents (or for old age grandparents) and ask them to relate their experiences to these periods.

Period		Tasks	Check	Statement
Infancy and Early Childhood (birth through preschool	1.	Achieving physiological rhythms in sleeping and eating	_____	
	2.	Learning to take solid foods	_____	
	3.	Beginning to relate emotionally to parents and siblings	_____	
	4.	Learning to talk	_____	
	5.	Learning to control elimination of body wastes	_____	
	6.	Learning to walk	_____	
	7.	Learning to distinguish right from wrong	_____	
	8.	Learning sex differences and sexual modesty	_____	
Middle Childhood (the elementary school period)	1.	Learning skills necessary for physical games	_____	
	2.	Building a positive self-concept	_____	
	3.	Adopting an appropriate masculine or feminine role	_____	
	4.	Learning to get along with peers	_____	
	5.	Developing values, a sense of morality, a conscience	_____	
	6.	Becoming personally independent, weakening family ties	_____	
	7.	Developing basic reading, writing, and arithmetic skills	_____	
	8.	Developing an understanding of the self and the world	_____	
Adolescence	1.	Developing conceptual and problem-solving skills	_____	
	2.	Achieving mature relationships with male and female peers	_____	
	3.	Developing an ethical system to guide behavior	_____	
	4.	Striving toward socially responsible behavior	_____	
	5.	Accepting the changing physique and using the body effectively	_____	
	6.	Preparing for an economically viable career	_____	
	7.	Achieving emotional independence from parents marriage and family life	_____	

Behavioristic Approaches to Development

6.   Behavioristic (learning-theory) approaches focus on immediate behavior and on environmental forces that affect behavior. In classical conditioning, a conditioned stimulus or CS (originally a neutral stimulus) is paired with an unconditioned stimulus or US (a stimulus that reliably brings about a response termed an *unconditioned response,* or UR) until presentation of the CS by itself is sufficient to bring about the response (now termed a *conditioned response,* or CR). Operant conditioning changes the probability of a response occurring as a function of its consequences. Positive reinforcers increase the probability of a response as a function of being added to a situation; negative reinforcers have the same effect when they are taken away from a situation. Punishment (adding something unpleasant or removing something pleasant) unlike negative and positive reinforcement, does not ordinarily increase the probability of a response, but has the opposite effect.

Exercise 6a: Mildred is upset because her child, Fennick is terrified of the house cat, Ginger. The cat seems so lovable that Mildred feels it just doesn't make sense that her baby is so frightened. Describe to this confused mother how the fear may have originated (using classical conditioning) and how the fear may be eliminated.

Exercise 6b: Using an operant conditioning approach explain to Ramona how she may be able to train her child, Gwendolyn from running out onto the street. (For the example use positive reinforcement only).

Exercise 6c: Felix just doesn't understand the difference between punishment and negative reinforcement. They seem the same to him. As simply as you can straighten out this issue for him.

Social-Cognitive Theory

7.   Bandura's theory of observational learning, which depends on attending, remembering, reproducing what is observed, and motivation, explains socialization as a function of imitation. Observational learning may be evident in the learning of new responses (modeling effect), the suppression or reappearance of deviant behaviors (inhibitory-disinhibitory effect), and the emission of behaviors similar but not identical to that of the model (eliciting effect).

Exercise 7a: Using Bandura's Theory of Observational Learning describe to Clyde why his child's watching 3 hours of violent television a day may be detrimental (modeling effect).

Exercise 7b: Your friend Belinda wonders if the company her children keeps has any effect on their behavior. Using Bandura's inhibitory-disinhibitory effect explain to her how peers can have an influence.

Exercise 7c: Make a self-efficacy check on your own accomplishments.

Enactive:
Vicarious:
Persuiasory:
Emotive:

A Cognitive Approach: Piaget

8.   Piaget's theory describes *cognitive* (intellectual) development in terms of adaptation resulting from interaction with the environment through using activities already in the child's repertoire (assimilation) and changing activities to conform to environmental demands (accommodation). The child's cognitive development is viewed as a sequential progression through four major stages; sensorimotor (world of here and now; intelligence in action), preoperational (egocentric thought; perception-dominated; intuitive rather than logical), concrete operations (logical thought operations applied to real objects and events), and formal (propositional thinking; potentially logical thought; hypothetical, idealistic reasoning).

Exercise 8: You are asked by a group of young mothers whether or not it is natural for their children to be continually "clinging" and hanging on to them or is there something wrong with their child. Using imprinting and Bowlby's concept of sensitive period, explain to them the biological view of bonding.

Biological and Ecological Approaches

9.   Vygotsky's cultural-historical approach emphasized the importance of culture and especially language. The *zone of proximal growth,* an expression of Vygotsky's belief in the interdependence of development and environment, is the child's potential for development in a given context. Bronfenbrenner's ecological systems theory looks at interactions and adaptations between the person and changing contexts at four levels: the microsystem (the child in face-to-face interaction), the mesosystem (interactions among contexts in the child's microsystem), the exosystem (interactions between one of the child's microsystem contexts and another context with which the child does not ordinarily interact), and the macrosystem (the totality of all cultural contexts relevant to the child's life).

Exercise 9a: Clenistine is eager for her child to start talking. Explain to her the 3 stages of speech according to Vygotsky and what is the function of these 3 stages.

Exercise 9b: Using Bronfenbrenner's Ecological Systems Theory give an example of each level in your own life.

<u>Personal Example</u>

Microsystem:

Mesosystem:

Exosystem:

Macrosystem:

Humanistic Approaches

10.   Humanistic theory is concerned with individual uniqueness, the importance of the individual's point of view (phenomenology), and human potential (self-actualization). Maslow describes two motivational need systems: *deficiency* (basic) needs, which are psychological (esteem, love) and physical (food, drink); and *metaneeds* (growth needs) such as the need to *self-actualize.*

Exercise 10:   Describe in one brief paragraph your concept of being self-actualized. In other words--what makes you unique--what is your personal view and how is that tied to your potential.

A Final Word About Theories

11.   People are more complicated than this chapter might suggest, but they are easier to understand within the context of the more organized systems or theories provided here than within the context of our naive intuitions. Although theories are never entirely wrong or right, they can still be useful.

Exercise 11:   Evaluate all of the theories presented by picking the 5 concepts that made most sense to you. See if you can tie them to YOUR theory.

I.   Reading and Understanding

Gene-Context Interaction
Chapter 3

This Chapter
--heredity
--environment
        --Heredity philosophers
Gene-Context Interactions
--Feral Children
--Genie: A Modern-Day Wild Child
Two Models of Gene-Context Relationships
--additive
--interactive
Interaction
--adaptive
--maladaptive
The Mechanics of Heredity
--Conception
        --ovum
        --sperm cell
        --conception
        --artificial insemination
--Sex Cells
        --puberty
        --menopause
--Carriers of Heredity
        --gametes
        --genetics
        --proteins
        --DNA
                --double helix
        --chromosomes
                --mitosis
                --mature
                --meiosis
--Sex chromosomes
        --autosomes
--Genes
        --genetic effects
        --gene functioning
                --dominant gene
                --recessive
                        --mutations
--Genotype and Phenotype
        --genotype
        --phenotype
                --dichotomous
                --normal curve
--Reaction Range and Canalization
        --canalized
        --The Epigenetic Landscape
        --Reaction Range
                --epigenesis
                --reaction range

--Molecular Genetics
      --Medelian genetics
            --restriction fragment length polymorphisms
                  --marker genes
Genetic Defects
      --recessive
      --dominant
--Huntington's Disease
--Sickle-Cell Anemia
      --heterozygous
--PKU
--Tay-Sachs Disease
--Muscular Dystrophy (MD)
      --Duchenne and Becker MD
--Neural Tube Defects
      --spina bifida
      --anencephaly
      --alphafetoprotein
--Diabetes Mellitus
--Nonmedical Conditions
Chromosomal Disorders
--Down Syndrome
      --Common Cause of Down syndrome
            --Trisomy
--Down Syndrome and Parental Age
--Abnormalities of the Sex Chromosomes
      --Turner's Syndrome
      --Klinefelter's Syndrome
      --XYY Males
      --Fragile X Syndrome
            --inherited
--Other Sex-Linked Defects
      --normal
      --carriers
Genetic Risk
--Fetal Diagnosis
      --Amniocentesis
            --amniotic fluid
            --alpha fetoprotein
--Chorionic Villus Biopsy (CVS)
--Ultrasound
      --sonogram
--Fetoscopy
--Radiography
--Preimplanatation Diagnosis
--Treating Genetic Disorders
      --possible
      --proven
--Genetic counseling
--The Future in Genetics
      --Rewriting Genetic Messages
      --Genetic Speculation
      --Ethical Issues
Studying Gene-Context Interaction
      --Genesis
            --interact
--Galton's conclusion
            --eugenics

--Animal Studies
        --Animal Studies of Gene-Context Interactions
        --Genetically Determined Behaviors in Humans
--Intervention Studies
        --The Sherman and Key Study
            --Mountain children
        --Head Start as Intervention
--Studies of Twins
        --monozygotic or identical twins
            --different egg cells
            --different spermatozoa
                dizygotic
        --Intelligence
        --Personality
--Adopted Children Studies
A final Look At Gene-Context Interaction
        --positivity
        --negativity
        --family context or family environment
        --monozygotic
        --dizygotic
        --full siblings
        -half siblings
        --unrelated siblings
--An Illustration of Gene-context Interaction
        --attractive
        --microsystem
        --mesosystem
        --exoystem
        --macrosystem
--Human Plasticity
        --rubber band hypothesis

II.   Learning and Comprehending

Scrambles
Chapter 3

Scramble 1:   Scrambled below are Genetic Defects and Chromosonal Disorders along with their descriptions. Place each abnormality in the appropriate column along with its description.

Genetic Defect - Description	Points	Chromosonal Disorder - Descriptions	Points
_____	_____	_____	_____
_____	_____	_____	_____
_____	_____	_____	_____
_____	_____	_____	_____
_____	_____	_____	_____
_____	_____	_____	_____
_____	_____	_____	_____
_____	_____	_____	_____
_____	_____	_____	_____
_____	_____	_____	_____
_____	_____	_____	_____
_____	_____	_____	_____
_____	_____	_____	_____
_____	_____	_____	_____
_____	_____	_____	_____
_____	_____	_____	_____
_____	_____	_____	_____
_____	_____	_____	_____
_____	_____	_____	_____
_____	_____	_____	_____
_____	_____	_____	_____

_____   _____   _____   _____

_____   _____   _____   _____

_____   _____   _____   _____

1. Tay-Sachs Disease
2. XYY males
3. Spine remains open at the bottom
4. Turner's Syndrome
5. Sickle-cell anemia
6. Males leave an extra Y chromosome
7. Fragile X Syndrome
8. Muscular dystrophy
9. Liver enzyme for breaking down phenylalenine absent or inactive
10. Abnormally shaped red blood cells
11. Anencephaly
12. "Mongolism" - mental retardation
13. Mothers with this disease have 2 to 3 times higher risk of birth defects
14. Klinefelter's Syndrome
15. Inability to walk
16. Huntington's Disease
17. Underdeveloped sex characteristics evidenced at puberty
18. PKU
19. Portions of the brain and skull are absent
20. Presence of both male and secondary sex
21. Enzyme disorder - break down certain fats
22. Spinal bifida
23. X sex chromosome is abnormally compressed or even broken
254. Diabetes mellitus
25. Rapid neurological deterioration after 30-40 years of age
26. Down's Syndrome

Scramble 2:   **Play the X and Y game. Match the appropriate letter(s) with the appropriate description.**

Letter	Description	Points
XYY	_____	_____
XY	_____	_____
Fragile X Syndrome	_____	_____
Y	_____	_____
XXY	_____	_____
XO	_____	_____
X	_____	_____
XX	_____	_____

Your Total Points _____
Total Possible Points 8
% = _____

1.   It's a girl!
2.   Super males
3.   Turner's Syndrome
4.   Carried by both males and females
5.   It's a boy!
6.   Klinefelter's Syndrome
7.   X chromosome compressed or broken
8.   Carried only by males

Scramble 3:   **Match the Fetal Diagnosis to the Appropriate Procedure**

Fetal Diagnosis	Procedure	Points
Ultra Sound	_____	_____
Radiography	_____	_____
Amniocentesis	_____	_____
Fetoscopy	_____	_____
Pre-implantation Diagnosis	_____	_____
Chorionic Villus Biopsy	_____	_____

Your Total Points   _____
Total Possible Points   40
% =   _____

1. Surgical procedure allowing physician to see fetus.
2. Determining chromosomal structure of fetus before the fertilized egg is implanted
3. Obtaining and examining fetal cells
4. Use of computer enhanced sound waves
5. Needle extracts I5-20 ml. of amniotic fluid
6. X-ray of fetus

Scramble Summary

		Your Points	Total Possible Points
Scramble I:	**Genetic and Chromosonal Disorder**	_____	26
Scramble 2:	**The X and Y Gene**	_____	8
Scramble 3	**Fetal Diagnosis**	_____	<u>6</u>

Your Total Points   _____
Total Possible Points   40
% =   _____

III.   Experiencing

Main Points and Exercises

Exercise
Chapter 3

Gene-Context Interactions

1.   The nature-nurture question asks about the interactions of genes and context that determine development. The older *additive* model assumed that genes contribute a certain percentage, and environment the remainder. The *interactive* model recognizes a more complex relationship between genes and environment, such that neither alone accounts for anything.

Exercise 1:   In considering your own inheritance list the characteristics you feel you inherited from your mother, father, be as detailed as possible. In doing this exercise you might wish to review characteristics of relatives on both sides as well (i.e., aunts, uncles, grandparents, etc.) which side do you feel has had more of an influence? Why?

Mother's Characteristics	Father's Characteristics	Mother's Relatives	Father's Relatives

The Mechanics of Heredity

2.   Conception, the beginning of life, requires the union of sperm and ovum. The bases of biological life are protein molecules made up of amino acids in complex arrangements determined by a special genetic code contained in sequences of deoxyribonucleic acid (DNA) molecules located on chromosomes. In the chromosomes are the carriers of heredity, the genes. Sex is determined by a special chromosomes labeled X and Y (XX equals female; XY equals male; only the father produces a Y).

Exercise 2.   The day has come that you knew would eventually arrive. Your child has asked you "Where do babies come from?" At a level you feel your child can understand, explain conception, DNA genes, chromosomes and heredity. This a tall order but you might relate what you were told as a child or what you would have wanted to be told?

2a.   Genetic makeup is *genotype; phenotype* refers to manifested characteristics. Genes, in pairs or in combinations of pairs, interact with the environment to influence certain characteristics. In major gene determination, characteristics corresponding to *dominant* genes will be manifested in the individual except where two recessive genes are paired. Manifested characteristics that correspond closely to underlying genetic makeup are said to be highly *canalized. Reaction range* refers to the range of possibilities implicit in genotype. Waddington's epigenetic landscape presents a analogy for understanding gene-environment interaction.

Exercise 2a: With every born child there is a tendency to make comparisons. "Oh, she looks like her dad." "He looks like his mom." In your own words, explain why this is using the information you learned about genotype, phenotypes, dominant and recessive genes, reaction range and canalization.

Genetic Defects

3.   Molecular genetics, which looks at the structure and function of genes, has located a large number of *marker genes*--specific segments of DNA that are associated with some identifiable characteristic. Many genetic defects are associated with recessive genes and will therefore not be manifested unless the individual inherits the genes (or gene combinations) from both parents. Huntington's disease (a fatal neurological disorder) is caused by a dominant gene. Sickle-cell anemia (the reduced ability of red blood cells to obtain oxygen), PKU (an enzyme disorder that sometimes leads to mental retardation), Tay-Sachs disease (another enzyme disorder leading to brain degeneration and death), and some forms of muscular dystrophy (a degenerative muscular disorder), diabetes (a sugar-processing disorder),   and neural tube defects are all examples of genetic disorders associated with recessive genes.

Exercise 3:   Select any of the genetic defects listed in the book and play the role of an M.D. describing to a parent specifically what has happened to produce the defect.

Chromosomal Disorders

4.   Chromosomal disorders result from errors in chromosomes and include down syndrome (Trisomy 21) and disorders associated with errors in sex chromosomes such as Turner's syndrome (linked to an absent sex chromosome); XYY syndrome (super males), affecting men only; Klinefelter's syndrome, affecting men with an extra X chromosome (XXY); and fragile X syndrome (a common cause of mental retardation especially among males).

Exercise 4:   Select any of the chromosomal disorders listed in the book and play the role of an MD describing to a parent specifically what has happened to produce the disorder.

Genetic Risk

5.   Some genetic abnormalities and fetal diseases can be detected prior to birth by means of amniocentesis (analysis of amniotic fluid withdrawn through a needle), chorion biopsy (analysis of preplacental tissue), fetoscopy (a surgical procedure to obtain fetal blood or skin samples), ultrasound (use of sonar techniques to detect physical characteristics and movement), radiography (X-rays), or preimplantation diagnosis (analysis of zygote cells prior to implantation). some genetic abnormalities and diseases can be treated or prevented; some can be detected before birth, or the risk of their occurrence can be estimated. There are some exciting and controversial possibilities in current genetics.

Exercise 5:   Your friend, Jane is pregnant and worries that there may be some genetic problems based on family history. She wonders what might be done. Explain to her the six different techniques mentioned in the book.

Studying Gene-Context Interaction

6.   Animal studies, as well as intervention studies with children (like Sherman and Key's study or research on Project Head Start), indicate that the environment influences characteristics such as intelligence. Twin studies and studies of adopted children corroborate these findings but also illustrate the importance of biology.

Exercise 6:   Fred is very intent on developing his newborn child's intelligence. He asks your opinion since you are taking the "Lifespan Development" course. Using the research on intelligence from animal and twin studies explain to him what influence he may have in expanding his child's IQ.

A Final Look at Gene-context Interaction

7.   Plomin and associate's study of mono- and fraternal twin pairs, as well as of siblings, stepsiblings, and nonrelated children, reveals that genes affect not only behavior but also environment (interactions in the family context, in this case). Elder's study of the differential impact of the Great Depression on the lives of attractive and less attractive girls also illustrates how biology (attractiveness) and the environment can interact to influence development. It is useful to emphasize the plasticity of, rather than the limits implicit in, our genes. The Stern hypothesis that genetic endowment is like a rubber band that assumes its final length--the actual performance of an individual--as it interacts with the environment, stressed the plasticity of our genes.

Exercise 7:   Write a personal paragraph on how you feel the genes you have inherited have interplayed with the environment. Select an area where plasticity is apparent.

I.   Reading and Understanding

Prenatal Development and Birth
Chapter 4

This Chapter
--artificial insemination
        --conception
Detecting Pregnancy
--pregnancy
--prenatal development
--menses
        --quickening
--stethoscope
Stages of Prenatal Development
--gestation period
--The Fetus
        --sucking reflex
        --Babinski reflex
        --lanugo
        --fertilized ovum or zygote
        --germinal stage
        --embryo stage
        --fetus
--Stage of the Fertilized Ovum
        --fertilization
        --Fallopian tubes
                --ovaries
                --uterus
                --placenta
                --umbilical cord
                --in utero
The Embryo
        --proximodistal
        --cephalocaudal
Factors Affecting Prenatal Development
--teratogens
--mutagens
        --cytomegalovirus
--Prescription Drugs
        --Frequency of Drug Use
        --Some Teratogenic Medical Drugs
                --thalidomide
                --quinine
                --barbiturates
                --anesthetics
                --aspirin
                --megadoses of vitamins
                --Diethylstilbestrol (DES)
        --Importance of Timing
--Chemicals
        --polychlorinated biphenyls (PCBs)
                --dioxin
                --methyl isocyanate
--Nicotine
--Caffeine

-Alcohol
    --Fetal Alcohol Syndrome (FAS)
        --fetal alcohol effects
    --Research on Maternal Drinking
    --How Much Can a Pregnant Woman Drink, and When?
--Substance Abuse
    --Narcotic
        --neonatal abstinence syndrome
    --Marijuana
        --Food and Nutrition Board, 1990
    --Cocaine
        --Sudden Infant Death Syndrome (SIDS)

    --Maternal health
    --Diabetes
    --Herpes
        cytomegalovirus
    --Acquired Immunity Deficiency Syndrome (AIDS)
--Maternal Emotions and Stress
--Older Mothers
--Teenage Mothers
--Maternal Nutrition
    --Effects of Serious Malnutrition
        --amenorrhea
--Effects of Stress Serious Malnutrition
--Nutritional Requirements during Pregnancy
    --Recommended Dietary Allowances, 1980
--Optimal Weight Gain
--Social Class
Rh(D) Immunization
    --Rh (or Rhesus) factor
    --immunization
    --fetal erythroblastosis
    --transplacental hemorrhage
--Preventing Rh(D) Immunization
    --Rhogam (Rh Immune Globulin or RhIG)
Childbirth
--What Starts It
--A Clinical View of Labor
    --Classifications of Birth
        --abortion
        --immature birth
        --premature birth
    --Small-for Gestational Age Infants
        --SGA
        --LGA
        --AGA
    --Stage I: Dilation
        --cervix
        --amniotic sac
    --Stage 2: Delivery
        --episiotomy
        --breech
        --transverse
    --Stage 3: The Afterbirth
        --neonate
        --afterbirth
        --dilation and curettage or D & C

--Cesarean Delivery
       Epidural analgesia
--Neonatal Scales
      --Apgar Scale
      --Brazelton Neonatal Behavioral Assessment Scale (NBAS)
--The Mother's Experience: Prepared Childbirth
      --Natural childbirth
          --Lamaze and Leboyer Methods
          --Hospitals or Homes: Doctors or Midwives
      --Sedatives in Childbirth
      --Postpartum Depression
--The Child's Experience
      --Dangers of Birth
          --forceps
          --anoxia
          --prolapsed cord
--Prematurity
      --Causes of Prematurity
      --Effects of Prematurity
      --Prevention of Prematurity
      --Care of Premature Infants
          --Nutrition and Medical Care
             --total parenteral nutrition (TPN)
          Psychological Care

II.   Learning and Comprehending

Scrambles
Chapter 4

Scramble 1:   **Listed below is the time of Prenatal Developmental Stages. List the appropriate stage and the description to the stage.**

Age	Stage	Description	Points
First 2 weeks	_____	_____	_____
Week two to week 8	_____	_____	_____
Week 8 to birth	_____	_____	_____

		Your Total Points	_____
		Total Possible Points	6
		% =	_____

1.   Period of the Fetus   a.   From the end of eighth week until birth. Accelerating growth curves toward the end of this period

2.   The Fertilized Ovum   b.   From end of second to end of eighth week of intrauterine development. During this stage most of the important morphological (pertaining to form) changes occur. *Teratogens* (influences that cause malformations and defects) are most influential during this period. At the end of this period, the embryo is close to 2 inches (4.5 cm) long and weighs about l/16 ounce (l9 grams).

3.   Embryo Stage   c.   Also termed the *geminal stage* or the period of the *zygote.* Begins at fertilization and ends with implantation of the zygote (fertilized egg) in the uterine wall about two weeks later. Still microscopic.

48

Scramble 2:   **Listed below are some teratogenic medical drugs. Match the drug to the potential physical changes.**

Drug	Potential Physical Changes	Points
Megadoses of vitamins (C,D,A,K, and B6)	_____	_____
Barbiturates	_____	_____
Quinine	_____	_____
Aspirin	_____	_____
Thalidomide	_____	_____
Anesthetics	_____	_____
DES (diethylstilbestrol)	_____	_____

Your Total Points _____
Total Possible Points 7
% = _____

1.   bleeding in mother and fetus
2.   physical changes in embryo
3.   birth defects
4.   depression of fetal respiration
5.   brain damage
6.   congenital deafness
7.   vaginal cancer in female offspring

Scramble 3:   **Listed below are 20 agents that may influence the fetus - Match the agent with influence.**

Agent	Influence	Points
1. Nicotine	_____	_____
2. Lithium carbonate	_____	_____
3. Radiation	_____	_____
4. Tetracycline	_____	_____
5. Iodine deficiency	_____	_____
6. Diabetes	_____	_____
7. Rubella	_____	_____
8. Caffeine	_____	_____
9. Vitamin A	_____	_____
10. (DES) diethylstilbestrol	_____	_____
11. Methylmercury	_____	_____
12. Alcohol	_____	_____
13. Polychlorinated biphenyls	_____	_____
14. Vitamin D	_____	_____
15. Herpes simplex	_____	_____
16. Radiation	_____	_____
17. Maternal starvation	_____	_____
18. Street drugs	_____	_____
19. Mechanical (constraint in the womb)	_____	_____
20. Thalidomide	_____	_____

Your Total Points _____
Total Possible Points   20
% =   _____

a. Fetal alcohol syndrome; intrauterine growth retardation; microcephaly; mental retardation
b. Anomalies of cervix and uterus; higher risk of cervical cancer
c. Heart and blood vessel defects; neural tube defects
d. Minimata disease; cerebral palsy; microcephaly; mental retardation; blindness; death
e. cola-colored children, gum, nail, and groin pigmentation; can affect offspring for up to four years after maternal exposure
f. Microcephaly; mental retardation, eye anomalies; visceral malformations
g. Fetal and pregnancy complications sometimes leading to death; no reported association with malformations
h. Tooth and bone staining if exposed during last two thirds of pregnancy
i. Limb reduction defects; anomalies of external ears, kidneys, and heart
j. Hypothyroidism of goiter; neurological damage
k. Defects involving limb development and position; neural tube, lip, palate, or abdominal defects
l. Intrauterine growth retardation; central nervous system anomalies; fetal death
m. Malformations involving internal organs; caudal dysplasia
n. Mental retardation; deafness; cardiovascular malformations; cataracts
o. Microcephaly; eye defects
p. Heavy use associated with lowered birthrate; no increase in malformation
q. Not likely to be a teratogen, although excess consumption may be toxic
r. Placental lesions; intrauterine growth retardation; increased mortality
s. Urogenital anomalies associated with massive doses; ear malformations; neural tube defects; cleft palate; facial abnormalities
t. Heart defects; facial malformation; mental retardation

Scramble 4

Listed below are the 3 scores of the Apgar Scale along with the 5 dimensions to be evaluated. Fill in the appropriate evaluation for each score level.

Score	Heart Rate	Respiratory Effort	Muscle Tone	Color	Reflex Irritability	Points
0	_____	_____	_____	_____	_____	_____
1	_____	_____	_____	_____	_____	_____
2	_____	_____	_____	_____	_____	_____

Your Total Points _____
Total Possible Points   15
% = _____

a. No response
b. Absent
c. Good, crying
d. flaccid, limp
e. Entirely pink
f. coughing, sneezing, crying
g. Slow (less than l00)
h. Blue, pale
i. Grimace
j. Rapid (over l00)
k. Absent
l. Strong, active
m. Irregular, slow
n. Weak, inactive
o. Body pink, extremities blue

Scramble Summary

Your Points

Scramble 1   **Prenatal Developmental Stages**   _____

Scramble 2   **Teratogenic Medical Drug**   _____

Scramble 3   **Agents That May Influence the Fetus**   _____

Scramble 4   **The Apgar Scale**   _____

Your Total Points   _____
Total Possible Points   **48**
% =   _____

III.   Experiencing

Main Points and Exercises

Exercises
Chapter 4

Detecting Pregnancy

1.   Early symptoms of pregnancy, such as cessation of menses, are uncertain, but simple chemical tests may be performed to detect changes in the woman's urine within a few weeks of conception. The gestation period for humans is 266 days (l0 lunar months from the onset of the last menses).

Exercise 1:   A young married couple (friends of yours) are looking forward to their first child. They want to know what they might look for in determining whether the mother is pregnant. Letting them know there are no "fool proof" signs mention several things listed in the book.

Stages of Prenatal Development

2.   Prenatal physiological development occurs in three stages: During the first two weeks, the *fertilized ovum* moves down the fallopian tubes and embeds itself in the uterine wall; from week 2 to week 8, the *embryo* develops so that by the end of the eighth week, all the organs of the infant are present; from week 9 until birth, the *fetus* grows mainly in size and weight and neurologically.

Exercise 2:   Loretta is pregnant and wants to know what is happening in the child's development. Write down a brief one sentence description of what is happening each month.

Month

1.

2.

3.

4.

5.

6.

7.

8.

9.

Factors Affecting Prenatal Development

3.   External influences that cause malformations and physical defects are labeled *teratogens. Mutagens* cause changes in genetic material. Effects of teratogens vary depending on genetic factors, the presence of other negative or positive influences, and their timing. Among teratogens are some prescription drugs (thalidomide or DES--linked with malformations and cancer); some chemicals (mercury--Minimata disease--and PCBs--linked with spontaneous abortions and physical deformities). Radiation can lead to spontaneous abortions and physical abnormalities.

Exercise 3:   You are a pediatrician who specializes in prescription drugs and how they effect prenatal development. You are asked to make a brief presentation to a group of expectant mothers and the influence of prescription drugs. In your own words what could you briefly tell them about: (see notes as guideline)

Thalidomide:

Quinine:

Barbiturates:

Anesthetics:

Aspirin:

Megadoses of vitamins C,D,A,K and B6:

DES (diethylstilbestrol):

3a.   Smoking cigarettes increases fetal heart rate and activity, and is associated with significant retardation of fetal growth, higher incidence of premature births, and higher risk of miscarriages and fetal death. Alcohol consumption may lead to fetal alcohol syndrome (FAS), symptoms of which may include mental retardation and characteristic cranial and facial malformations. Infants born to narcotic addicts are themselves usually addicted at birth; in severe cases, they may die. In addition, narcotics such as heroin and opium are associated with prematurity. Stimulants such as cocaine may also be associated with prematurity, lower birthweight, and developmental problems.

Exercise 3a: You have some friends who are "at risk" potential parents. (involved in smoking, alcohol, and street drugs). If the conversation would come up, what would you tell them about the effect of any (or all) of the following on their potential offspring.

Smoking:

Alcohol:

Narcotics:

Marijuana:

Cocaine:

3b.   Various maternal diseases and infections such as rubella, syphilis, gonorrhea, and diabetes can lead to mental deficiency, blindness, deafness, or fetal death. Herpes can be transmitted to the fetus during birth and can lead to serious complications including death. AIDS can also be transmitted from mother to fetus (35-60 percent probability) and is fatal.

Exercise 3b: Blanche desperately wants to having children but her family seems to continually come up with every disease in the book. What would you tell her if she asked you about diseases and having children. Obviously, you cannot tell her about every disease but to get the idea across you might want to cover the following diseases.

Rubella (German measles):

Syphilis:

Gonorrhea:

Diabetes:

Herpes:

AIDS:

3c.   There is a higher probability of some chromosomal defects such as Down syndrome and fragile X syndrome for older parents. Infants born to teenage mothers are at higher risk of physical, emotional, and intellectual disadvantage (more miscarriages, premature births, and stillbirths, and more emotional and physical abuse among those who survive--outcomes associated more with the social and medical circumstances of teenage parenthood than with the mother's age). Famine and malnutrition may lead to lower fertility rates and higher fetal mortality. Social class, because of related medical, nutritional, and drug use factors, is associated with a higher incidence of prematurity and other complications.

Exercise 3c: You are a genetic counselor at a local community hospital. A couple over 45 wish to have a child. What would you tell them about Tresony 21 and l8 and how they are related to:

Down syndrome:

Fragile X syndrome:

Klinefelter's syndrome:

Neural tube defects:

Congenital heart disease:

Growth retardation:

What would you tell them about Chorion biopsy and amniocentesis procedures in coping with the potential difficulty?

3d.   In the absence of medical intervention, mothers who are negative for the Rh blood factor, where the father is Rh-positive, would be a risk of giving birth to infants suffering from fetal crythroblastosis. This condition is routinely avoided in modern hospitals through use of the drug Rhogam.

Exercise 3d: Sara is a pregnant teenage neighbor who knows you are going to college and taking this course. She asks you what you know about pregnant teenagers. Describe what you would tell her along with information that might be of help in overcoming the problems.

Exercise 3e: Phil has just found out he is to become a father. He surprises you with the following question. "What do you know about this Rh stuff? My wife's parents mentioned it and we have to see a doctor." What could you tell him about the Rh factors and how it relates to Rhogam.

Childbirth 4.   Expected rate of birth is 266 days after conception. Early deliveries are termed *premature* (before the 37th week). Newborns are also classified as small-for-gestational age (SGA) if they weight l0 percent less than average newborns of the same gestational age. Birth occurs in the three stages: labor (dilation of the cervix, about 912 hours), the actual delivery (about l hour), and the afterbirth (the expulsion of the placenta and other membranes, several minutes). Cesarean deliveries has increased dramatically in recent years largely as a result of improved technology for fetal monitoring. Newborns are routinely evaluated at birth by means of the Apgar scale--a scale that looks at their Appearance (color), Pulse (heart rate), Grimace (reflex irritability), Activity (muscle tone), and Respiration (respiratory effort) (note the mnemonic, or memory, device).

Exercise 4:   You are asked by a friend, "How can the hospital know if my kid is normal?" You describe to the Apgar scale.

A (   )

P (   )

G(   )

A(   )

R(   )

Notice the mnemonic device; a technique you can use for memorizing most material.

4a.   Natural, or prepared, childbirth (Lamaze or Leboyer, for example) refers to the preparation for and process of having a child with little or no use of anesthetics. Birth poses two great dangers for the neonate: The first is cerebral hemorrhage, resulting from extreme pressures in the uterus or in the birth canal; the second is prolapse of the umbilical cord and shortage of oxygen.

Exercise 4a: Your friend, Bennie tells you his wife is going to have a child and they are going to use natural childbirth. Then he says, "I'm going to be part of the program. We are going to use the Lamaze or Leboyer method. What is that anyway?" Describe to him each technique.

Prematurity

5.   Prematurity appears to be linked to social-class variables such as diet and poor medical attention, to the age of the mother, and to smoking. Its most apparent effects are the greater possibility of death, physical defects, hyperactivity, and impaired mental functioning. Medical advances have made it possible for more than 90 percent of premature infants weighing as little as l,000-1,500 grams (l/2-2/3 pounds) to survive. The severity of possible medical consequences of prematurity has been significantly ameliorated by medical advances. In addition, the psychological consequences of prematurity can be offset through increased tactile (stroking, cuddling), auditory, vestibulatory (rocking), gustatory (pacifier), or multimodal stimulation. Still, many premature infants suffer physical or mental handicaps.

Exercise 5:   You are shocked to find out that your first child is born prematurely. Relate each of the three classifications of birthweight on what you might expect and how you might treat your child.

Exercise 5a: This would be an excellent time to explore what you have been told about your own birth. Ask your parents or if that's not possible ask your relatives who might know something. Write a page or two about yourself and how you entered the world. Listed below are some questions that might stimulate some thinking and questions of your own.

Where were you born?

What time of the day?

Were you planned or spontaneous?

Who named you? How?

Were there any special circumstances?

Was the birth smooth? or did things unexpectedly happen?

What was the thing most notable to your mother? Father?

What was your grandparents reaction? Your relatives?

Now its your turn for questions.

Physical and Cognitive Development: Infancy
Chapter 5

This Chapter
The Newborn
--neonate
Health and Physical Growth
       Breast Versus Bottle
       Human Growth
            --Genital Growth
            --Pubescence
            --Lymphoid Growth
            --Neural Development
            --Physical Growth
Sudden Infant Death
       -sudden infant death syndrome (SIDS)
--What is SIDS
       --Some Common Characteristics
       --SIDS and Neurological Immaturity
            --apnea
       --Preventing SIDS
            --triple-risk model
Behavior in the Newborn
--The Orienting Response
       --galvanic skin response (GSR)-(electrodermal response)
--Reflexes
       --sucking reflex
       --vegetative reflex
       --head-turning reflex
       --rooting reflex
       --Moro reflex
       --Palmar reflex (Darwinian reflex)
Motor Development
       --cyclic movements
            --sensorimotor
            --cephalacaudal
            --proximodistal
Perceptual Development
       --sensation
       --perception
       --conceptualization
--Infant vision
       --vision at birth
       --color and movement
            --pupillary reflexes
       --depth perception
--Visual preferences
       --faces versus blanks
       --attractive versus ugly
--How infants look
       --Infants look to see
            --fovea
            --maximize neural firing
       --Rules that guide infant looking

--Hearing
      --discriminating voices
--Smell, Taste, and Touch
      --pain sensitivity
      --the state of the neonate
Cognitive Development
      --information-processing
--Infant memory
      --studying infant memory
          --habituate
      --developmental phases in infant memory
          --organization, grouping, and elaboration
--Basic Piagetian Ideas
      --here and now
      -Assimilating and Accommodating
          --schema
          --equilibration
      --factors that shape development
          --construction
          --maturation
          --active experience
          --social interaction
--The Object Concept
      --here and now
      --objective objects
--Discovering that things are real
--Piaget's classic object concept study
--Piaget underestimated infants
--Sensorimotor Development
      --exercising reflexes (birth to l month)
      --primary circular reactions (l to 4 months)
      --secondary circular reactions (4 to 8 months
      --purposeful coordinations (8 to 12 months)
      --tertiary circular reactions (12 to 18 Months)
          --tertiary
      --mental representation (18 months to 2 years)
          --cognitive
          --mentally
--Imitation in Infancy
      --imitation in very young infants
          --deferred imitation
      --imitation in older infants
          --familiar
      --achievements of imitation in infancy
          --familiar social behavior
          --new social behaviors
Language
--Communication
--A Definition of Language
      --language
      --displacement, meaning, and productiveness
      --psycholinguists

--Elements of Language
       --phonology
       --phonemes
       --morphemes
       --semantics
       --syntax
       --pragmatics

Language Development in Infants
       --active vocabulary
       --passive vocabulary
--Achievements in the Prespeech Stage
       --simple representation
       --symbolic representation
--Language Origins
       --language acquisition support system (LASS)
--Turn-Taking
       --Gestures
--First Sounds
       --sound discrimination
       --sound production
           --babbling
           --stop, glide, or nasal
       --the first word
--The Sentencelike Word (Holophrase)
       --holophrase
--Two-Word Sentences
       --baby talk
       --telegraphic speech
       --early grammar
From Sensation to Representation
       --sensorimotor

II.   Learning and Comprehending

Scrambles
Chapter 5

Scramble 1   **Match each statement with the appropriate statistic.**

Statement	Statistic	Points
Do not survive beyond age 1	_____	_____
Usually die from congenital anomalies	_____	_____
Sudden Infant Death Syndrome (SIDS)	_____	_____

	Your Total Points	_____
	Total Possible Points	3
	% =	_____

1.   5500 infant deaths in l991
2.   9 of l000 infants (40,000)
3.   6 (2/3's) of 1000 infants

Scramble 2   **In the appropriate time sequence match the reflex with the Stimulus and Response**

Reflex	Stimulus	Response	Points
_____	_____	_____	_____
_____	_____	_____	_____
_____	_____	_____	_____
_____	_____	_____	_____
_____	_____	_____	_____
_____	_____	_____	_____
_____	_____	_____	_____
_____	_____	_____	_____
_____	_____	_____	_____
_____	_____	_____	_____
_____	_____	_____	_____

Your Total Points   _____
Total Possible Points   36
%=   _____

1.   Placing object in the infant's hand
2.   Babinski reflex
3.   Sucks
4.   Swimming reflex
5.   Grasps object tightly
6.   Toe grasp
7.   Moro reflex
8.   Swallows
9.   Irritation in the nasal passages
10. Object placed against both of infant's palms
11. Babkin
12. Object in the mouth
13. Spreads and raises toes
14. Sudden loud noise
15. Food in the mouth
16. Swallowing
17. Turns head toward side from being stroked
18. Infant's head turned to one side
19. Tonic neck
20. Sneezes
21. Coordinated swimming movements
22. Head-turning (rooting)

23. Stepping reflex
24. Opens mouth, closes eyes, turns head to the side
25. Infant horizontal, supported by abdomen
26. Tickling the middle of the soles of the feet
27. Sucking
28. Throws arms and leg out symmetrically
29. Palmar grasp
30. Stroking the cheek or the corner of the mouth
31. Infant vertical, feet lightly touching flat surface
32. Arm and leg extend on that side, flex on opposite side
33. Curls toes around object
34   Tickling the soles just below the toes
35. Makes coordinated walking movements
36. Sneezing

Scramble 3   **In the appropriate time sequence match the reflex with the approximate Age of Appearance - Age of Disappearance**

Reflex	Approximate Age of Appearance	Approximate Age Disappearance	Points
_____	_____	_____	_____
_____	_____	_____	_____
_____	_____	_____	_____
_____	_____	_____	_____
_____	_____	_____	_____
_____	_____	_____	_____
_____	_____	_____	_____
_____	_____	_____	_____
_____	_____	_____	_____
_____	_____	_____	_____
_____	_____	_____	_____

Your Total Points _____
Total Possible Points 36
% = _____

1.   8-9 months in utero
2.   Sneezing
3.   Becomes voluntary during first year
4.   Neonate
5.   Sucking
6.   Neonate
7.. Disappears after 2-3 months
8.   Late fetal period
9.   Toe grasp
10. Babkin
11. Palmar grasp
12. Neonate
13. 4-6 months in utero
14. 8-9 months in utero
15. tonic neck
16. 4-6 months in utero
17. Swimming reflex
18. Babinski reflex

19. Neonate
20. Head-turning (rooting)
21. Neonate
22. Swallowing
23. Stepping reflex
24. 2-3 months in utero
25. Becomes voluntary during first year
26. Disappears by 9 months
27. Disappears by 4 months
28. Disappears after 6 months
29. 4-6 months in utero
30. Becomes voluntary during first year
31. 3-4 months
32. Moro reflex
33. Diminishes by I month; disappears by 5-6 months
34. Disappears after 4 months
35. Weak by 8 weeks; gone by 4-5 months
36. Disappears by 9 months

Scramble 4   **Match the Rule that Guides Infant Looking (p.15)**

Rule	Guide	Points
Rule 1	_____	_____
Rule 2	_____	_____
Rule 3	_____	_____
Rule 4	_____	_____

Your Total Points   _____
Total Possible Points   4
% =   _____

1.   If in light with no form, search for edges using broad, jerky sweeps of the field
2.   If in darkness, maintain a controlled, detailed search.
3.   If an edge is found, terminate the broad scan and stay in the general vicinity of that edge. Try to implement eye movements that cross the edge. If such eye movements are not possible in the region of the edge (as is the case for edges too distant from the center of the field), scan for other edges.
4.   If awake and alert and light not too bright, open eyes.

Scramble 5   **Match each of the four forces that accounts for the construction of knowledge with the appropriate definition. (Oh yes, may the FORCE be with you).**

Force	Description	Points
_____	_____	_____
_____	_____	_____
_____	_____	_____
_____	_____	_____

Your Total Points   _____
Total Possible Points   8

1.   Maturation
2.   The tendency to balance assimilation (responding in terms of previous learning) and accommodation (changing behavior in response to the environment
3.   Social Interaction
4.   Interaction with real objects and events allow individual to discover things and to invent (construct) mental representations of the world

5.   Genetic forces that do not determine behavior but are related to its sequential unfolding
6.   Equilibration
7.   Interaction with people leads to the elaboration of ideas about things, people, and self
8.   Active Experience

Scramble 6   **Put together the Stage, Approximate Age and some major Characteristics of Piaget's Theory of Cognitive Development**

Stage	Approximate Age	Some Major Characteristics	Points
_____	_____	_____	_____
_____	_____	_____	_____
_____	_____	_____	_____
_____	_____	_____	_____
_____	_____	_____	_____
_____	_____	_____	_____
_____	_____	_____	_____
_____	_____	_____	_____
_____	_____	_____	_____
_____	_____	_____	_____
_____	_____	_____	_____
_____	_____	_____	_____

Your Total Points   _____
Total Possible Points   12
% =   _____

1. Understanding of number
2. 7 to 11-12 years
3. Formal operations
4. Egocentric thought
5. Concrete operations
6. Complete generality of thought
7. 11-12 to 14-15 years
8. Sensorimotor
9. 0-2 years
10. Preoperational
11. 2-7 years
12. World of the here and now

Scramble 7

Listed below are the Sex Substages of sensorimotor development. Put them in the Appropriate Time Order along with the Appropriate Characteristics

Substage and Approximate Age in Months	Principle Characteristics	Points
_____	_____	_____
_____	_____	_____
_____	_____	_____
_____	_____	_____
_____	_____	_____
_____	_____	_____
_____	_____	_____
_____	_____	_____
_____	_____	_____
_____	_____	_____
_____	_____	_____
_____	_____	_____

Your Total Points _____
Total Possible Points 12
% = _____

1. Activities that center on the infant's body and that give rise to pleasant sensations are repeated (thumb-sucking, for example)
2. Purposeful coordinations (8-12)
3. Exercising reflexes (0-1)
4. Transition between *sensorimotor* intelligence and a more *cognitive* intelligence; activity is internalized so that its consequences can be anticipated before its actual performance, language become increasingly important in cognitive development
5. Activities that do not center on the child's body but that lead to *interesting* sights or sounds are repeated (repeatedly moving a mobile, for example)
6. Secondary circular reactions (4-8)
7. Simple, unlearned behaviors (schemes) such as sucking and looking are practiced and become more deliberate
8. Mental representation (l8-21)
9. Separate schemes become coordinated (such as the ability to look at an object and reach for it); recognition of familiar people and objects, primitive understanding of causality begins, implicit in the use of signs to anticipate events
10. Tertiary circular reactions (12-18)
11. Repetition with variation (repeating a sound with a number of deliberate changes, for example) is experimented with
12. Primary circular reactions (1-4)

Scramble 8

In accurate chronological order match the correct stage in a child's development of grammar to the nature of development.

Stage of Development	Nature of Development	Points
_____	_____	_____
_____	_____	_____
_____	_____	_____
_____	_____	_____
_____	_____	_____
_____	_____	_____
_____	_____	_____
_____	_____	_____
_____	_____	_____
_____	_____	_____
_____	_____	_____

Your Total Points _____
Total Possible Points 12
% = _____

1. Elements are added, embedded, and permuted within sentences. Word classes (nouns, verbs, and prepositions) are subdivided. Clauses are put together.
2. Multiple-word sentences (by 2 to 2 1/2 years)
3. Crying, cooing, babbling
4. Two-word sentences (duos) (by l/2 years)
5. Modifiers are joined to topic words to form declarative, question, negative, and imperative structures
6. Prespeech (before age 1)
7. Complex structural distinctions made, as with "ask-tell" and "promise"
8. More complex grammatical changes and word categories (between 2 1/2 and 4 years)
9. Both a subject and predicate are included in the sentence types. Grammatical morphemes are used to change meanings (*ing* or *ed*, for example).
10. Adultlike structures (after 4 years)
11. The word is combined with nonverbal cues (gestures and inflections)
12. Sentencelike word (holophrase) (by 1 year)

66

Scramble Summary

Scramble 1	Children's Survival Rate	_____
Scramble 2	Reflex, Stimulus, Response	_____
Scramble 3	Reflex, Age of Appearance	_____
Scramble 4	Rules for Infant Looking	_____
Scramble 5	Construction of Knowledge	_____
Scramble 6	Theory of Cognitive Development	_____
Scramble 7	Six Substages of Sensorimotor Development	_____
Scramble 8	Development of Grammar	_____

Your Total Points   _____
Total Possible Points 123
% =

III.   **Experiencing**

Main Points and Exercises

Exercises
Chapter 5

The Newborn

1.   A new born is a primitive, self-driven little sensing machine designed to mature and grow physically in a predetermined sequence and at a relatively predictable pace, programmed as an extraordinarily capable information-processing system, endowed with powerful gregarious tendencies and strong emotions, and pretuned to the development of language.

Exercise 1:   In a dyad or small group situation try to communicate your needs to someone (or your group) without speaking or pointing. Be the newborn trying to communicate. After exchanging with another (or your group) see if you can come up with a list of how the newborn tries to communicate.

Health and Physical Growth

2.   Human breast milk is infant-specific, easily, digested, nourishing, useful in guarding against the possibility of diarrhea, and provides a degree of immunity to infant illnesses. Genital growth is minimal in infancy (until pubescence); lymphoid and neural growth occurs very rapidly; optimal brain development is profoundly influenced by nutrition (especially protein) and stimulation; and physical growth is relatively rapid (it slows through middle childhood and spurts again at adolescence).

Exercise 2a.   Since breast feeding is such an issue determine if you want breast feeding as part of your children's upbringing. Depending upon your sex determine the answer to the following questions.

Females - do you want to breast feed your child?

Yes (why)?

No(why)?

Advantages

Disadvantages

<u>Males</u> - do you want the mother of your children to breast feed?

Yes (why)?

No (Why)?

Advantages

Disadvantages

Exercise 2b. <u>Role Play</u> - In a dyad of female-male role play the discussion of whether or not to breast feed. Role play where both agree and alternate when one agrees and the other disagrees (i.e., female wants to and male doesn't want you to; then alternate female doesn't want to, male thinks it is a good idea). Use the information in Exercise 2a as a guide.

Exercise 2c. Discuss with your mother whether or not you were breast fed. How was the decision made? What were some memories they had in feeding you?

Exercise 2d. Although this may be highly personal and you need not share it with anyone try to remember your first awareness of sexuality during your pubescence period. Can you relate or answer any of the following questions -- were you frightened? confused? Were you able to talk to your parents about it? did you talk to your peers -- or did your peers talk to you? did you feel quilt, embarrassed, self conscious? What other feelings did you have? What did you to about the feelings?

Sudden Infant Death

3.   Sudden infant death syndrome (SIDS) accounts for the unexpected and largely inexplicable deaths of apparently healthy infants. It is more common among males, rarely occurs after the age of 6 months, and is sometimes associated with factors such as neurological immaturity, sleeping in a prone position, a mild upper-respiratory infection, apnea, lower Apgar scores, or other factors, none of which have been shown to cause SIDS.

Exercise 3   You have just become a proud parent. Based on what you have learned from the Lifespan Development Text explain to your mate SIDS, the common causes and what you can do to prevent it.

Behavior in the Newborn

4.   The orienting response (for example, changes in heart rate or respiration) is a useful measure of interest, attention, and learning in infants. The behavioral repertoire of the neonate consists largely of reflexes (for example, sucking, Moro, Babinski, Palmar (grasping), swimming, stepping, swallowing, and sneezing). Many of these disappear with the development of the brain and the achievement of voluntary control over movements.

Exercise 4a.   In order to understand reflexes pair off with another classmate. Take turns being parent and child. Alternating roles the parent conducts the following action and the child relates their response.
a.   Tickle under the chin
b.   Stroke the right or left cheek
c.   Touch the right or hot side of the neck
d.   Touch the nostrils
e.   Place finger gently inside the ear.
Take turns in relating the experience to one another.

Exercise 4b.   To get a feeling for an automatic response perform a task usually administered by a medical doctor. Gently tap the region below your knee cap and feel the response of your leg.

Secondly, with your shoes and socks off gently draw a semicircle on the bottom of your foot. Try to reproduce the Babinski reflex. Congratulations - you have been able to relive very early childhood memories.

Motor Development

5.   Infants engage in regular, cyclic motor activities. The development of motor skills seems to be governed by two principles: cephalocaudal (head to tail) and proximodistal (near to far).

Exercise 5   List 5 males and 5 females you feel are attractive. Give a different reason for each. Now meet in a small group. compare your list with others. Come up with characteristics in which you all agree. Discuss attractiveness and the kinds of facial feature you consider attractive.

Perceptual Development

6.   Visual capacities (color, motion, depth) are well developed in the newborn. The infant's looking seems to be directed by rules that maximize information. Neonates are only slightly less sensitive than adults to sound intensity (loudness). They appear to recognize and prefer their other's voices at ages as young as 3 days. They prefer pleasant odors (such as vanilla) to those less pleasant (ammonia or raw fish) almost from birth. Similarly, they prefer the sweet to the bland, they distinguish easily between sour and bitter tastes, and they appear to be sensitive to touch (and to pain), at least within a few hours of birth.

Exercise 6a.   Two of your friends get into an argument over whether an infant "knows" their mother. They turn to you, being the experiment is in lifespan development to answer the question. Based on what is contained under perceptual development for the infant knowing the mother is it all hogwash?

Exercise 6b.   A young couple wants to know how much and how fast their newborn is learning. Relate to them each of the senses and what seems to be the evidence for learning as an infant.

Cognitive Development

7.   The neonate's memory is not as efficient, as powerful, or as long-term as that of older children or adults, but there is memory for smells and sights within days of birth. By the age of 3 months, infants actively search and show signs of recognition.

Exercise 7   Greg feels it is nonsense that infants have a memory. Explain to him the 3 ways they have been able to demonstrate that infants do have memories. You can even dazzle him with the word habituation to prove your point.

8.   In Piaget's theory, adaptation (cognitive growth) results from the interplay of assimilation (responding in a habitual and preferred way based primarily on preexisting information and well-practiced capabilities) and accommodation (adapting behavior to some external characteristic or quality). Equilibration is the tendency to balance assimilation and accommodation. Other important factors in cognitive development are maturation, social interaction, and active experience. Piaget's six substages of the sensorimotor period are (1) exercising reflexes, (2) primary circular reactions, (3) secondary circular reactions, (4) purposeful coordinations, (5) tertiary and (6) mental representation

Exercise 8. You fancy yourself as an expert on Piaget's Theory. At a family meeting some relatives are talking about young children and learning. You immediately dazzle them with your knowledge about the 4 forces that accounts for the construction of knowledge. Outline below the four forces and what you would say. (You might also rehearse what you would say when they mention how brilliant you are).

9. There is increased frequency of simple infant behaviors like tongue protrusion following exposure to a model, even in very young infants. It is not entirely clear that these are always imitative behaviors. Evidence of deferred imitation is seen by the age of 9 to 12 months; it depends on the ability to represent mentally and to remember, and is therefore of considerable importance in cognitive development.

Exercise 9. Again, as a Piagetian expert explain to Gloria and Phil, a young couple, soon to be parents, what they can expect to be learning over the first two years. Mention also what they can expect their child to be doing. Use the 6 substages of the sensorimotor stage as an outline.

Language

10. Language involves the use of arbitrary speech sounds that have accepted meanings. It is characterized by displacement, meaningfulness, and productiveness. Its elements are phonology, semantics, syntax, and pragmatics.

Exercise 10 Imagine yourself as a child learning to speak. Listen to a foreign language tape or talk to someone who speaks a foreign language. List 10 new phonemes. Now find out what it means (semantics). Put several of these together to make a sentence with meaning (syntax). Try to put several together to made additional sentences. You are now an infant level in a new language.

Language Development in Infants

11. Infants discriminate sounds at very young ages; also, they are able to produce many sounds in their babbling. Babbling becomes systematic by the age of 7 to 10 months. Linguistic experience eventually modifies the infant's ability to discriminate and to produce sounds. The ability to use and understand words grows out of a complex series of interactions between parents and young infants. Infants as young as 2 months have a relatively sophisticated awareness of the turn-taking signals used in conversation.

Exercise 11   Check with your parents to find out what were the first words you spoke (beside mama and dada). How did they teach you to speak? What were some surprising words you uttered that your parents remembered? What were some special words you used that they remember?

12.   In the prespeech stage (first year of life), the infant coos, gurgles, cries, and babbles. Two important achievements of this stage are the development of the intention to communicate and the discovery that things have names. The first meaningful word appears around age 1, and is often sentencelike in nature(a holophrase). Two-word sentences (telegraphic, highly condensed) appear around the age of 18 months, at which time there is a spurt in vocabulary growth.

Exercise 12   Check with your parents about your baby talk, What were some twisted words, phrases or expressions? Explain to your parents the term holophrase. Ask them what holophrases you used. Relive those early moments of communication with your parents.

I.   Reading and Understanding

Social Development: Infancy
Chapter 6

This Chapter
Interactions in the Family Context
--Beyond the Dyad: A Model of Influences
      --meso--, exo--, and macrosystems
--How Infants Influence Parents
Infant States
      --rapid eye movements (REM) sleep
      --infancy
      --infant state
Temperament
--Types of Infant Temperament
--Classifying Temperament
      --Early Infancy Temperament Questionnaire
      --Revised Infant Temperament Questionnaire
The Implications of Infant Temperament
      --Implications for Parenting
Cultural Context and Temperament
      --goodness-of-fit
Infant Emotions
--Crying
      --Kinds of Infant Cries
            --rhythmic cry
            --hunger cry
--Smiling and Laughing
      -anencephalic
--Wariness and Fear
      --learned fears
--Why Infants are Sometimes Afraid
Regulation of Emotions in Infancy
--How Infants Control Their Emotions
      --self-directed behaviors
      --other directed regulatory behaviors
Early Attachment
--Studying Attachment
      --Ainsworth's Strange Situation
            --strange situation
            --securely attached
            --insecurely attached
            --insecure-avoidant
            --insecure-ambivalent
            --disorganized/disoriented
Mother-Infant Bonding
      --Attachment
            --mother-infant bond
            --Ethologists
            --critical period
            --failure to thrive (FTT) - (maternal deprivation syndrome)
      --Bonding Mechanisms
            --preadaptations
            --cyclical motor movements
--The Importance of Bonding

--Stages of Attachment
    --Preattachment
    --Attachment in the Making
    --Clear-Cut Attachment
    --Goal-Corrected Attachment
--The Implications of Attachment Patterns
--Fathers and Infant Attachment
    --Fathers as Parents
Fear of Strangers and Separation from Parents
    --separation protest
--Fear of Strangers
    --mutism
    --incongruity hypothesis
--Separation Anxiety in Other Cultures
    --multiple caregiving
--Preventing Stranger Anxiety
--Security Blankets
    --transitional objects
        --individuation
--Longer-Term Separation from Parents
Infant Care
Parenting in Infancy
    --attentiveness
    --physical contact
    --verbal stimulation
    --material stimulation
    --responsive care
    --restrictiveness
--Cultural similarities
Early Gender-Role Influences
    --gender roles (or sex roles)
    --Gender typing
--When does Gender typing Being
Exceptionality
--The Lifespan
--Motor Skill Disorders
    --developmental delays
--Cerebral Palsy
    --significant developmental motor disability
        --dyskinesia
        --orofacial praxis
--Other Motor Skill Disorders
    --developmental coordination disorder
        --Diagnostic and Statistical Manual of Mental Disorders (DSM-III-R)
            --developmental coordination disorder
--Epilepsy
    --grand mal
    --petit mal
    --benign infantile epilepsy
--Other Physical Problems
--autism
    --pervasive developmental disorder
The Whole Infant

II.   Learning and Comprehending

Scrambles
Chapter 6

Scramble 1:   **Match the Infant Temperament with the Description and the Approximate Percentage**

Temperament	Description	Approximate Percentage	Points
_____	_____	_____	____
_____	_____	_____	____
_____	_____	_____	____

Your Total Points   _____
Total Possible Points   9

1. Regularity in eating and sleeping (high rhythmicity); high approach tendencies in novel situations; high adaptability to change; preponderance of positive moods; low or moderate intensity of responses
2. Difficult
3. 10
4. Irregularity to eating and sleeping (low rhythmically); withdrawal in novel situations; slow adaptation to change; preponderance of negative moods; high intensity of reactions to stimulation
5. 40
6. Easy
7. Slow to warm up
8. Low activity level; high initial withdrawal from unfamiliar; slow adaptation to change, somewhat negative mood; moderate or low intensity of reaction to stimulation
9. 15

Scramble 2:   **Listed below are 4 attachment classifications. Match the appropriate common behavior when mother leaves or returns**

Attachment Classification	Common Behavior When Mother Leaves or Returns	Points
Insecure ambivalent	_____	_____
Securely attached	_____	_____
Disorganized/Disoriented	_____	_____
Insecure Avoidant	_____	_____

Your Total Points   _____
Total Possible Points   4

1. Rarely cries when mother leaves; ignores or actively avoids her when she returns, sometimes pushing her away or pointedly not looking at her
2. Contradictory, disorganized reactions to separation and reunion; may cry for mother but run away when she returns, or approach her while looking away
3. Uses mother as a base from which to explore; upset when she leaves but quickly soothed when she returns, greets her positively on return
4. Very upset when mother leaves; often angry when she returns, sometimes pushing her away

Scramble 3:   **In the Appropriate Time Sequence organize the phase, Approximate Age and Important Behaviors.**

Phase	Approximate Age	Important Behavior	Points
_____	_____	_____	_____
_____	_____	_____	_____
_____	_____	_____	_____
_____	_____	_____	_____

Your Total Points _____
Total Possible Points   12

1.   Continued use of behaviors designed to draw attention--smiling, crying, squirming, use of newly developed locomotor skills to approach attachment object or person
2.   Into second half of first year
3.   Crying, smiling, rooting, clinging, sucking, looking at; movements synchronized with adult speech; discrimination of mother's voice
4.   Attachment in the making
5.   Second half of first year
6.   Clear-cut attachment
7.   Singling out objects of primary attachment; selective social smile--directed more toward attachment objects or persons than toward the unfamiliar
8.   Second year
9.   Preattachment
10. First Month
11. Goal-corrected attachment
12. Begins to adopt mother's point of view and to make inferences about mother's behavior; manipulation of mother's behavior in more subtle ways following gradual recognition of cause-and-effect relationships

Scramble 4:   **Match the category of cerebral palsy (classified by body function) with the appropriate description.**

Category	Body Function	Points
_____ Tremor	_____	_____
_____ Mixed	_____	_____
_____ Rigidity	_____	_____
_____ Spastic	_____	_____
_____ Atoxia	_____	_____
_____ Athetosis	_____	_____

Your Total Points _____
Total Possible Points 6

1. Characterized by loss of control over voluntary muscles. Movements tend to be jerky and uncontrolled. Some symptoms in two out of five cerebral palsy victims
2. Involves shaky movements, most often of the hands, sometimes visible only when the individual is voluntarily attempting to do something involves less extensive movement than athetosis or spasticity
3. Marked by trembling, drooling, facial gestures, and other involuntary and purposeless muscle activity (fluttering of the hands, for instance--in contrast with the rigid, jerky movements of spasticity). Often affects speech as well. Frequently found in combination with spasticity. Affects one out of five cerebral palsy individuals.
4. Manifested in balance problems and an uncertain walk. Affect approximately one out of four of those with cerebral palsy
5. Involves a combination of characteristics descriptive of one or more of the common classifications. Most cerebral palsy victims fall within this category, although the majority are described in terms of their most predominant characteristics
6. Caused by strong opposing tension of flexor and extensor muscles, resulting in fixed and rigid bodily postures (sometimes referred to as *lead pipe cerebral palsy*)

Scramble Summary

Your Score _____
Total Possible Score 31

Scramble 1	**Infant Temperaments**	_____	_____
Scramble 2	**Types of Infant Attachment**	_____	_____
Scramble 3	**Sequential Phases in the Developmental of Infant Attachment**	_____	_____
Scramble 4	**Categories of Cerebral Palsy**	_____	_____

Your Total Points _____
Total Possible Points 31
% = _____

III.   Experiencing

Main Points and Exercises

Exercises
Chapter 6

Interactions in the Family Context

1.   Influence in infant-parent interactions is bidirectional and strongly affected by the characteristics of both parent and infant (the microsystem) as well as by the larger context.

Exercise 1   Ask your parents how your birth had an influence on each of them. How did it influence the family, in other words, describe the contextual model and how your birth had an influence.

Infant States

2.   Infant states reflect basic individual differences very early in life. Common infant states include regular sleep, irregular sleep, drowsiness, alert inactivity, alert activity, and crying.

Exercise 2   Find out from your parents what infant states they remember during your early months. Using Wolf's 6 distinct infant state category -- where would you fall. If you were the parent how would you hand this state (after all it may happen).

Temperament

3.   Individual personality differences among infants define temperament, which is assumed to have a strong genetic basis. Three broad infant temperaments are difficult, easy, and "slow to warm up." In North America, "easy" may be an advantage. The infant's temperament may contribute to developmental outcomes by affecting how parents interact with it and how they feel about themselves as parents. Also "goodness-of-fit" between the infant's temperament and environmental demands may affect developmental outcome.

Exercise 3   Based on what you have been told about your early years would you say your temperament was easy-difficult-slow to-warm up? Discuss this with your parents. Discuss with them also the goodness-of-fit concept. How did they react to your temperament?

Infant Emotions

4.   Infant's facial expressions and other behaviors reveal a number of distinct emotions. Some of which are evident in infant crying (rhythmical, hunger, anger, and pain). The reflexive smile is often present only hours after birth; the social smile (often in response to a human voice) is uncommon before the age of 3 weeks; by 4 months, infants also laugh. Both crying and smiling progress from responses to internal stimuli to external stimuli. Fear responses occur most often in the fact of the unexpected. Fear of strangers is not common before the age of 6 months and appears to be related to the infant's ability to distinguish between the familiar and the unfamiliar. Infant control over emotions may be through *other-directed regulatory behaviors* (smiling, for example) and *self-directed regulatory behaviors* (thumb-sucking, for example).

Exercise 4   Explain to an expectant mother the different types of cries that may be anticipated and what they mean.

Early Attachment

5.   Forming an attachment with a caregiver is one of the most important tasks of early infancy. (*Bonding* refers to the biologically based processes by which parents and infants form attachment links.) Ainsworth's Strange Situation procedure identifies *securely attached* infants (use mother as exploration base; upset when she leaves; react positively to her return); and *insecure-avoidant* (rarely cry when mother leaves; ignore or avoid her when she returns (or *insecure-ambivalent* (very upset when mother leaves; often angry when she returns). *Disorganized/disoriented* infants display a range of disorganized behaviors (crying at the door but withdrawing when parent returns).

Exercise 5   Madonna just doesn't know why her child Dennis reacts that way when she is gone for brief moments. Explain to her the attachment classifications and the common behaviors that might be anticipated.

6.   There appear to be powerful genetic tendencies toward the formation of caregiver-infant bonds (evident, for example, in infants' preference for the human voice and human face, as well as in response tendencies such as rooting and sucking reflexes). Infant attachment to the mother appears to be important to the healthy development and adjustment of the infant. Four sequential phases in the development of attachment are preattachment (first month); attachment in the making (into second half of first year: selective social smile); clear-cut attachment (after 6 months: use of motor skills to approach attachment object); and goal-correct attachment (second year: more subtle manipulation of attachment person's behavior). Infants appear to become equally attached to their mothers and fathers when given the opportunity to do so.

Exercise 6a   Penelope is about to have her first child and wants to make sure she and the child will be close. Describe to her attachment phases, approximate ages and the behavior she might anticipate.

Exercise 6b   This exercise has 2 parts. The first part is to write down the role that your father played in your upbringing. How closely were you attached? List the things you did together? How would you classify the relationship-Close/Some close-Some distant/Distant

The second part of the exercise depends upon your being a female or male.

For Females

-----What role do you see the father of your child taking?

-----For Males

----What role do you see yourself taking in the upbringing of your children?

For both of the above relate specifics and give some practical examples.

Will it make a difference if it is a female or male child? If so how?

Fear of Strangers and Separation from Parents

7.   Fear of strangers is uncommon before 6 to 9 months and may result from *incongruity* between expectations and reality. Infants who have experience with siblings and strangers are less prone to stranger anxiety. Transitional objects such as blankets and teddy bears are sometimes effective in reducing anxiety in some stressful situations. Longer-term separation from the primary caregiver leads to disturbances in most infants after the age of 6 months.

Exercise 7a   Discuss with your parents your reaction to strangers. Were you frightened? bold? Withdrawn? Unaffected? Did you have a household where many people came to visit or the family was isolated? Do you feel that has influenced your reaction to strangers today, i.e., do you like to meet new and different people or are you shy?

Exercise 7b   Did you have anything near a security blanket, like a toy Teddy bear, Barbie doll, etc.? Do you still have it? (or even remember or think about it?)

Infant Care

8.   High-quality infant care does not appear to disrupt parent-infant bonds or to prevent their formation and has no consistent negative effects.

Exercise 8   Harry and Harriette cannot make ends meet without both of them working. They seek your advice as a family counselor (you have decided on this profession because of the Lifespan Development course you took in college). Based on the material you have read what would you tell them?

81

Parenting in Infancy

9.   Among important dimensions of parenting in infancy are attentiveness, physical contact, verbal stimulation, material stimulation, and responsive care--each of which has positive effects on the infant's social and intellectual development--and restrictiveness, the effects of which are more negative.

Exercise 9   Briefly jot down your impressions of your mother and your father. List l0 adjectives that describe each. Do they match the stereotype mentioned in your book i.e., mother affectionate, warm, less strict than father. Check your adjective list and descriptions to see where they are the same as Western society and where they are different.

Early Gender-Role Influences

10.   From the moment of birth, a subtle process of gender typing begins. Many mothers and fathers react differently to male and female children, interact with them differently, have different expectations of them, and perceive them differently.

Exercise 10a   Although the following questions might be delicate to discuss with your parents you might want to explore them just to see how it might have influenced your child rearing.
A.   Did your parents want a boy or girl? Or did it matter?

B.   Did you fulfill that gender role?

C.   Did they have names picked out - male - female - what were they?

D.   Did they paint the room, buy new toys or take an other action before your birth? Did it have a gender bias (i.e., painting the room pink)

E.   Do YOU have a preference for your first child? What and Why?

Exercise 10b. Did you ever wish you were born the opposite sex? Why? If you could --
magically change --what would life be like?

Exceptionality

11.   Exceptionality has both positive and negative dimensions, and may be evident in cerebral
palsy, epilepsy, a variety of diseases, congenital physical problems or physical problems resulting
from accidents. Emotional exceptionality may be apparent in childhood-onset pervasive
developmental disorders (like autism), which are rare but very serious early forms of emotional
disorders.

Exercise 11.   Select any one of the 3 forms of exceptionality in your book - cerebral palsy,
epilepsy or autism. Describe to a friend the most obvious symptoms and what might be done
about it.

I.   Reading and Understanding

Physical and Cognitive Development: Early Childhood
Chapter 7

This Chapter
Physical Growth
Motor Development
--Developmental Timetables
--Motor and Intellectual Development
--Motor and Social Development
The Preschooler's Mind
--Infantile Amnesia
The Preschooler's Memory
--Incidental Mnemonics
--Preschoolers' Memory Strategies
      --deliberate
      --systematic
--Development of Early Memory Strategies
      --metamemory
Piaget's View
--sensorimotor intelligence
--preoperational
      --operation
      --preconceptual
      --intuitive
--Preconceptual Thinking
      --Preconcepts
         --concepts
         --preconcepts
            --transductive reasoning
         --syncretic reasoning
      --Transductive Reasoning
         --deduction
         --induction
      --Syncretic Reasoning
--Intuitive Thinking
      --intuitive
      --egocentric
      --perception-dominated
      --classification errors
--An Example of Intuitive Thinking
      --intuitive
--Classification Problems of the Preschooler
--Preschooler Egocentricity
      --egocentric
      --egocentric speech
--Reliance on Perception
      --conservation
--Replications of Piaget's Work
      --underestimates
      --Was Piaget Wrong
--Cognitive Achievements of the Preschooler
      --Number Concepts
         --number abstraction skills
         --numerical reasoning principles
         --count

Preschool Education
--Nursery Schools
--Compensatory Programs
        --Project Head Start
        --Good Compensatory Programs
                --family as a child-rearing unit
                --Montessori method
        --Some traditional Montessori materials
--Kindergartens
Language and the Preschooler
--Language Development in Infancy
        --duos
--Multiple-Word Sentences
--More Complex Changes
        --conjunction
        --embedding
        --permutation
--Adultlike Structures
Explanations of Language Development
--The Role of Biology
        --The Evidence for Biology
                --language acquisition device (LAD)
        --Genie's Story
--The Role of Early Experience
--Parents as Teachers
        --Child-Directed Language (Motherese)
A Changing Language Context
--Different Views of Bilingualism
        --Substractive bilingualism
        --Addictive bilingualism
                --transitional bilingualism
        --Transitional bilingualism
                --balanced bilinguals
        --Subtractive bilingualism
                --subtractive
        --Additive bilingualism
        --Which View Is Correct?
--Bilingualism in Today's Schools
        --inclusive
        --The Other Side
                --English Only
                --English First or U.S. English
Speech and Language Problems
Language, Thought, and Communication
--Thinking and Language
        --Whorfian
        --Pensees
--Communicating and Conversing

85

II.   Learning and Comprehending

Scrambles
Chapter 7

<u>Scramble 1:</u>   **List 3 Gross Motor Tasks and 4 Fine Motor Tasks and the Approximate age at which children accomplish the task.**

<u>Gross Motor Task</u>	**<u>Approximate Age (90%)</u>**	**<u>Points</u>**
_____	_____	_____
_____	_____	_____
_____	_____	_____

<u>Fine Motor Task</u>	**<u>Approximate Age (90%)</u>**	**<u>Points</u>**
_____	_____	_____
_____	_____	_____
_____	_____	_____
_____	_____	_____

Your Total Points   _____
Total Possible Points   14

1.   Balances on 1 foot 1 second
2.   16.3 mos.
3.   Tower of 8 cubes
4.   23.2 mos.
5.   Balances on 1 foot 5 seconds
6.   4.6 yrs.
7.   Draws person, 6 parts
8.   3.4 yrs.
9.   Scribbles
10.   5.4 yrs.
11.   Kicks ball forward
12.   3.5 yrs.
13.   Draws person, 3 parts
14.   5.6 yrs.

Scramble 2: **List 5 Physical Characteristic at each of the years listed below.**

At 2 years begins to	At 3 years begins to	At 4 years begins to	At 5 years begins to	Points
_____	_____	_____	_____	_____
_____	_____	_____	_____	_____
_____	_____	_____	_____	_____
_____	_____	_____	_____	_____
_____	_____	_____	_____	_____

Your Total Points _____

Total Possible Points 20

1. Skip
2. Walk a reasonably straight path on floor
3. Run, jump, and climb with close adult supervision
4. Stand on balance beam
5. Reproduce alphabet and numbers
6. Copy figure X
7. Stand on one foot for a short time
8. Sit in a chair without support
9. Jump rope, walk in a straight line
10. Walk down stairs alone
11. Copy figures 0 and +
12. Push and pull
13. Slide
14. Walk on balance beam
15. Walk balance beam with ease
16. Gain good body control
17. Dress self using buttons, zippers, laces, and so on
18. Catch
19. Hop
20. Fold paper

Scramble 3   **Listed below are the 5 Stages of Early Development of Memory Strategy. Match them appropriately.**

Memory Strategy	Early Development of memory Strategy	Points
Stage 1	_____	_____
Stage 2	_____	_____
Stage 3	_____	_____
Stage 4	_____	_____
Stage 5	_____	_____

Your Total Points   _____
Total Possible Points   5

1. In the early elementary school years, children use somewhat more effective strategies, but are often distracted by irrelevant information
2. In the beginning, the infant doesn't deliberately use strategies to remember
3. Later, strategies become increasingly effective and are applied in a variety of settings.
4. The preschooler may occasionally use primitive strategies, but these don't always result in memory improvement
5. Finally, as a result of repeated practice with memory strategies, their use becomes habitual and automatic

Scramble 4   You have already been introduced to and had a scramble on Piaget's Stages of Cognitive Development. Without reading your previous scramble or referring to the book, see how many of the following you can fill in correctly.

Stage	Approximate Age	Two Major Characteristics		Points
_____	_____	_____	_____	_____
_____	_____	_____	_____	_____
_____	_____	_____	_____	_____
_____	_____	_____	_____	_____

Your Total Points _____
Total Possible Points 16

1. 0-2 years
2. Preoperational
3. Propositional thinking
4. Inability to conserve
5. Sensorimotor
6. Thinking bound to concrete
7. Motoric intelligence
8. Reason dominated by perception
9. Development of strong idealism
10. 7 to 11-12 years
11. 11-12 to 14-15 years
12. Concrete operations
13. 4-7 years
14. Logic of classes and relations
15. Formal operations
16. 2-7 years

Scramble Summary

		Your Points
Scramble 1	**Gross and Fine Motor Tasks**	_____
Scramble 2:	**Physical Characteristics**	_____
Scramble 3:	**Stages of Early Development of Memory Strategies**	_____
Scramble 4:	**Piaget's Stages of Cognitive Development**	_____

Your Total Points _____
Total Possible Points 55
% = _____

III. Experiencing

Main Points and Exercises

Exercises
Chapter 7

Physical Growth

1.   There is a gradual slowing of sheer physical growth after fancy. In addition, different parts of the body grow at different rates (the head grows more slowly, for example) so that a typical 6-year-old looks more like an adult (and less like an infant) than a 2-year-old does.

Exercise 1:   Claire and Harry are about to have their first child and are interested in physical changes in the first few years of a newborn. Explain to them how their child will change physically, using for example the proportions of the head to body size (Figure 7.4)

Motor Development

2.   Among significant motor achievements of infancy are learning how to walk and to coordinate other motor activities. Motor, intellectual, and social development are very closely related.

Exercise 2a.   Let's play a little game. You are asked to do a test called the Draw-A-Person test. Draw a person as a preschooler and a child who is now in First grade. Using the information contained on pages ( ) ( ) what would the figures look like? What might be expected and not expected?

Exercise 2b. Titus has strong ambitious to have his son Titus II be an outstanding athlete so at one month he is already teaching the child how to catch a football. Brenda, Titus' wife wants you to explain the physical characteristics and development to him and explain why the child will probably not sign a professional sports contract by age 10. (Use Table 7.2 as a guide and good luck)

Exercise 2c: Take the information on Table 7.2. Check with your parents what they remember of each of the physical characteristics and the years in which they began (i.e., when did you first learn to what, how, what circumstances?) You might want to write up these memories so you may share them with others -- perhaps your own children. It will also give you a chance to reminisce with your parents and perhaps uncover some old "special moments."

The Preschooler's Mind

3.   We remember little of personal experience of infancy and the early preschool period (*infantile amnesia*). Preschoolers' memories result largely from *incidental mnemonics* (paying attention, repeated exposure) rather than from the deliberate use of strategies (such as organizing or rehearsing). However, older preschoolers may deliberately use strategies when instructed to remember something, although these are sometimes inappropriate.

Exercise 3   This section introduces mnemonics, a valuable tool in taking exams. Let's go through a practical example, one which you may use with a number of other courses beside this one. Write down each of the stages listed for the early development of memory strategies. Now select one (or at the very most two) words for each stage. Make some sort of sentence out of these words. When you are asked a question about the stages, all you have to do is unravel the sentence--put it at the appropriate stage and PRESTO you know the stages and the strategies. Now you have an idea of how mnemonics (even complicated mnemonics) work.

Piaget's View

4.   Piaget's preoperational period includes *preconceptual thinking* (2-4: classification errors, preconcepts, and transductive and syncretic reasoning) and *intuitive thinking* (4-7: egocentricity, errors of class inclusion, and a marked reliance on perception). Piaget's developmental sequence has often been replicated although he seems to have underestimated ages of attainment in some cases. The neo-Piagetians present a somewhat more optimistic view of the preschool child, emphasizing that one of the major achievements of this period is the ability to relate one or more ideas or concepts.

Exercise 4:   Kirk thinks his 2-year-old, Fabian is dumb because all the birds he sees flying he calls Robins. Explain to Kirk, Piaget's stage of cognitive development especially syncretic reasoning.

5.   As a result of their ability to relate concepts, preschoolers can classify and solve simple class-inclusion problems, have a remarkable understanding of number that reflects both number abstraction skills (understanding numerosity, based on universal counting principles) and numerical reasoning (understanding of some of the effects of transformations), and have made enormous strides in language learning.

Exercise 5   John is convinced his preschooler Maurice is a mathematical genius because of how he handles numbers. Explain to him what might he anticipate of a preschooler in understanding numerosity and numerical reasoning. Is his child outstanding or just what kids that age can do?

Preschool Education

6.   Preschool education programs include nursery schools, day-care centers, compensatory programs, and a variety of other approaches. In general, compensatory preschool programs (Head Start, for example) have measurably positive effects on cognitive and social development, as do regular kindergartens. However, some fear that emphasis on formal instruction at the preschool level hurries children unnecessarily and robs them of their childhood.

Exercise 6:   Gil and Angela are split on whether or not they should send their child to preschool. they keep mentioning the Montessori method. Present to them the pro and con debate about preschool mentioning the "College Degree" and "Gold Medal" parent.

Language and the Preschooler

7.   Language--the use of arbitrary sounds with established and accepted referents, either real or abstract, that can be arranged in sequence to convey meaning--appears to be unique to humans. The child goes from one-word sentences (holophrases) to two-word sentences (duos) and then to multiple-word sentences (rather than simply to three-word sentences). Multiple-word sentences appear by age 2 to 2 1/2 and make extensive use of grammatical morphemes such as *ing* and *ed* to convey meaning. More complex sentences and adultlike grammatical structures are typically present by age 4.

Exercise 7:   Phil and Di have a 1 1/2 year old they keep correcting and wonder if she will ever speak in full sentences. Explain to them the last 3 stages in the development of grammar especially the more complex changes of conjunction, embedding and permutations.

Explanations of Language Development

8.   Imitation and reinforcement are not completely adequate explanations for the observation that the earliest speech sounds of all infants are very similar, that infants make few directly imitative mistakes as they learn language, and that there appears to be a critical period for language learning early in life (as Genie's story illustrates). Chomsky advances the metaphor of a language acquisition device (LAD), which suggests that children learn language as if they were neurologically predisposed to do so.

Exercise 8:   How would you defend the biological stage of language development (Chomsky) if you got into a big debate with someone who firmly believed language was totally a learned phenomenon and you could teach anyone to speak at any time?

9.   The mother (and other caregivers) play an important role as language teacher, unconsciously fine-tuning her speech patterns to a level just in advance of that of her child. Thus, *motherese* is characterized by shorter sentences, more repetition, simpler and more concrete concepts, and exaggerated intonation.

Exercise 9:   Did your mother use "motherese" to teach you to talk? If you don't know ask her; in fact if your dad or even a relative used "motherese". Find out how they used it.

A changing Language Context

10.   Changing demographics are rapidly changing the language composition of North American countries, although bilingualism is often *transitional,* lasting only three or four generations. Learning two languages may sometimes be a *subtractive* experience (especially when minority-language speakers are schooled exclusively in a more socially valued majority language), or an *additive* experience (more common when a minority language is learned as a second language in a school immersion setting).

Exercise 10:   Imagine that for some reason (marriage, a job, a job transfer) you must now learn a second language. What would be your response (thoughts, feelings, attitude, etc) How would you approach the task of learning a new language?

Exercise 10b. Find someone from your friends or classmates who speaks more than one language. Ask them the questions debated in the book (i.e., subtractive vs. additive). What is your personal opinion based on exercises 9 A and B?

Speech and language Problems

11.   The language sophistication of most school-age children is sufficient for them to ask and answer questions, tell stories, follow instructions, engage in conversations, and so on. However, some children experience language and speech problems ranging from complete absence of speech and comprehension to minor articulation and voice problems. These problems may be related to mental retardation, neurological damage or disease, or mental disorders, and are sometimes associated with adjustment problems in school and society.

Exercise 11:   For an experience in a speech problem try talking to yourself on some topic for five minutes. Do this aloud (but find a safe place). Now stutter repeatedly during the allotted time. Did you find it difficult? Did you even embarrass yourself? How did you feel about it? How would you feel if you couldn't control it and were actually talking to someone? (Try a mirror for instance.) Perhaps this off beat exercise can give you some empathy for an individual with a speech difficulty.

Language, Thought, and Communication

12.   Evidence suggests that language sophistication can contribute significantly to higher mental thought process. The strong version of the Whorfian hypothesis maintains that language precedes and is necessary for thought. A weaker version is that language influences thought. Piaget and Vygotsky note evidence of thought prior to language (and in nonhuman animals). One of the major social functions of language is to enable communication through conversation.

Exercise 12:   Recall your last conversation with a child (age 1 1/2 to 4). Did you recognize any of the concepts mentioned in this chapter? Did you modify your language? Did they repeat yours? To what degree do you think you were conversing - none, a little, a lot? To what degree were you communicating - none, a little, a lot? Now that you know this chapter will it help? What will you change?

I.   Reading and Understanding

Social Development: Early Childhood
Chapter 8

This Chapter
Social Development
      --Socialization (or social learning)
--Erikson's Psychosocial Stages
      --psychosocial development
      --trust versus mistrust
      --autonomy versus shame and doubt
            --intentionality
      --initiative versus guilt
            --autonomous self
--Social Imitation
      --imitation
      --identification
            --modeling effect
            --inhibitory and disinhibitory effects
--Cooperation and Competition
      --A Cross-Cultural Illustration
      --Observational Learning in Complex Societies
Preschoolers' Emotions
--Interpreting Emotions
      --social referencing
--Regulating Emotions
      --expression
      --self-directed regulatory behaviors
      --other-directed regulatory behaviors
--Emotional Expression
      --display rules
Play
--Functions of Play
      --Practice Play (or sensorimotor play)
      --Imaginative play
            --thinking
--Practice Play
--Pretend Play
      --Reality and Fantasy
            --pretend
      --Daydreaming and Imaginary Playmates
      --Contributions to a Theory of Mind
            --states of mind
            --theory of mind
            --metacognition
--Social Play
      --Solitary play
      --Onlooker Play
      --Parallel Play
      --Associative Play
      --Cooperative Play
--Cultural Differences in Play
Gender Roles in Early Childhood
      --masculine or feminine
      --gender roles
      --gender typing
      --Developing Gender Schemas and Stereotypes

--Two Theories
        --Stage 1. Basic gender identity
        --Stage 2. Gender stability
        --Stage 3. Gender constancy
--Gender Differences and Stereotypes
    --stereotypes
    --Sex Differences in Play
    --Genetic Influences
    --Sociocultural Models and Expectations
The Contemporary Family
    --nuclear
    --extended
--Parenting in Early Childhood
    --sustenance
    --advocacy
    --attentiveness
    --physical contact
    --verbal stimulation
    --material stimulation
    --responsive care
    --absence of restrictiveness
    --Parenting styles
    --Permissive parenting
    --Authoritative parent
    --Novice and Expert Parents
--Do Parents Make a Measurable Difference
    --Conflicting Findings
    --Baumrind's Advice
        --specific
    --authoritative
    --Child-Care Advice
--Learning How to Parent
    --intergenerational transmission of parenting styles
    --Sources of Child-Care Advice
Family composition
    --Birth Order
    --Family Size
    --Age Intervals
One-Parent Families
    --Do Separation or Divorce Have Negative Effects?
    --Age- and Sex-related Effects of Divorce
--Why Divorce or Separation Might Have Negative Effects
    --Father (or Mother) Absence
    --Economic Impact
    --Family Conflict
    --Parental Disengagement
        --independent variable
        --dependent variable
--Less Negative Effects of Divorce
--Resolving the controversy
--A Final Word
Children in Stepfamilies
    --blended families
    --stepfamily
--Possible Problems in Stepfamilies
--The Positive Side

NonParental Child Care
--General Effects of Child Care
        --family child care
        --Child Care versus Home Care
        --Specific Effects of Child Care
            --quality
            --poorer quality
--Finding Quality Child Care

II.   Learning and Comprehending

Scrambles
Chapter 8

Scramble 1: **Fill in the appropriate Erikson Stage, Approximate Age and Two Principle Developmental Tasks in the correct age sequence.**

<u>Stage</u>	<u>Approximate Age</u>	<u>Two Principle Developmental Tasks</u>		<u>Points</u>
_____	_____	_____	_____	_____
_____	_____	_____	_____	_____

Your Total Points   _____
Total Possible Points   8

Stage
1.   Autonomy vs. shame and doubt
2.   Initiative vs. guilt

Approximate Age
1.   2-3 to 6 years
2.   18 months to 2-3 years

Principal Development Task
1.   Developing a greater sense of responsibility for own actions
2.   Learning that one is autonomous, that intentions can be realized
3.   Developing a sense of self-largely through identifying with parents
4.   Developing a sense of control and master over actions

Scramble 2:   **Match the Appropriate Play with correct classification**

Classification	Possible Activity	Points
_____	_____	_____
_____	_____	_____
_____	_____	_____
_____	_____	_____
_____	_____	_____
_____	_____	_____

Your Total Points   _____
Total Possible Points   12

Classification
1. Associative play
2. Primitive social play
3. Onlooker play
4. Cooperative play
5. Parallel play
6. Solitary play

Possible Activity
1. "Peek-a-boo"
2. Two children play with dolls, talk with each other about their dolls, lend each other diapers and dishes, but play independently, sharing neither purpose nor rules
3. Two children play with trucks in sandbox, but do not to interact. They play beside each other, but not together.
4. Child watches others play "tag" but does not join in
5. Child plays alone with blocks
6. "Let's pretend. You be a monster and I'll be the guy with the magic sword and..."

Scramble 3

Listed below are parenting styles and some characteristics. Match 3 characteristics for each style.

Style	Characteristics			Points
Authoritarian	_____	_____	_____	_____
Permissive	_____	_____	_____	_____
Authoritative	_____	_____	_____	_____

Your Total Points _____
Total Possible Points 9

1. Permits independence but values obedience
2. Obedience highly valued
3. Self-control and autonomy limited
4. Nonpunitive
5. Imposes regulations, but allows discussion
6. Nondemanding
7. Based on reason
8. Very controlling
9. Autonomy more important than obedience

Scramble 4: Fill in the sentence with the appropriate statistic

		Points
1.	_____% of white parents that will divorce before child is 16 years of age	_____
2.	About _____ of mothers of preschoolers now work	_____
3.	_____ of family care is by grandparents and other relatives	_____
4.	About _____ of U.S. women went back to work one year after giving birth.	_____
5.	_____% of black parents that will divorce before child is 16 years of age	_____
6.	_____ of single-mother families are below poverty level	_____
7	_____ of first marriages end in divorce	_____
8.	Of households that had families _____ of the black households were single parents	_____
9.	_____ of step family marriage end in divorce	_____
10.	Of households that had families _____ of the Hispanic were single parents.	_____
11.	Of households that had families _____ of the whites were single parents	_____

Your Total Points _____
Total Possible Points 11

50	75
60	57.5
46	18
31	60
52	38
75	

Scramble Summary

		Points
Scramble 1	**Erikson's Stages**	_____
Scramble 2	**Play**	_____
Scramble 3	**Parenting Styles**	_____
Scramble 4	**Conditions-Frequency**	_____

Your Total Points _____
Total Possible Points 40
% = _____

III.   Experiencing

Main Points and Exercises

Exercises
Chapter 8

Social Development

1.   Erikson's stage theory of social development describes the resolution of psychosocial conflicts through the development of competence. Stage 3, *imitative versus guilt,* spans the preschool period, and involves developing a sense of personal agency and accepting responsibility for one's actions. Bandura's theory of social development holds that much social learning takes place through observational learning (imitation), including acquiring such socially important characteristics as the tendency to cooperate or to compete, which are highly influenced by the individual's immediate culture.

Exercise 1:   Your neighbor Fay has an easy going cooperative preschool child but each time she meets with a relative who has a child of the same age they end up in a tug of war. She asks you "What's wrong with that kid?" Explain to her the cooperation and competition research mentioned in the chapter and how it may relate to her circumstance.

Preschoolers' Emotions

2.   Socializing emotions requires learning how to interpret feelings (sometimes using *social referencing)* , achieving some control over them (through *other-* and *self-regulatory behaviors*), and learning rules of emotional display.

Exercise 2:   Try to recall the earliest experience you had in discovering display rules, especially when you expressed an emotion different from your underlying feelings. As an adult are there any consistent circumstances that require you to react to the display rules in this same way?

Play

3.   Practice play may be useful for developing and exercising important physical skills, as well as for establishing social position and teaching acceptable forms of behavior. Pretend play is closely related to cognitive development and the development of the child's *theory of mind*. Social play underlies personality development and the development of social skills. Infants as young as 1 year are often capable of pretend play (for example, pretending to be asleep or pretending to eat). Later, during the preschool period, boys' pretend play often involves monsters or superheroes; girls' pretend play is often more concerned with home-related or nurturant themes. Daydreaming and imaginary playmates are forms of pretend play. Social play, which involves interaction among two or more children, may be onlooker play (looking without joining in), parallel play (laying independently side by side), associative play (playing together without sharing rules), or cooperative play (sharing of rules and goals).

Exercise 3a: Recall 3 of the earliest games you played. Who did you play with (or did you play alone)? What were the rules? Did it involve winning and losing or just accomplishing a task?

Exercise 3b: Ask your parents about the earliest games they played with you. What was your response? How did they teach you? What were the rules? Did you play primarily with mother? father? both? Have them recall your play history?

Gender Roles in Early Childhood

4.   Gender roles, the range of behaviors and personality traits that are considered appropriate for males and females (that are *masculine* or *feminine*) result from an interaction of genetic and contextual forces. Sex differences in childhood are evident in the tendency of boys to play more physically, in the toys they select and are given, and in the roles they assume in their pretend games (these differences are more apparent later rather than earlier in the preschool period). A cognitive explanation for gender typing describes three stages: recognizing basic gender identity (maleness or femaleness); realizing that gender is stable, permanent, and unchangeable; and realizing that superficial changes, in dress or behavior, for example, do not alter gender.

Exercise 4:   Recall your earliest memory regarding gender differences. How did you become aware of it? Did you discuss it with your mother and father? What were your initial reactions. Recall the females that were classified as tomboys. Why were they given that label? What did they do? [for females] Did you participate in any of that behavior? Did you want to? Recall the males that were classified as sissies. Why were they given the label? What did they do? [For males] Did you participate in any of that behavior? Did you want to?

5.   Genetic influences on gender differences are especially evident in the greater aggressiveness of males. Contextual influences are reflected in the fact that most parents treat boys and girls differently--rewarding aggression, independence, and boisterousness in boys, and nurturant, affective, complaint behavior in girls.

Exercise 5:   Your text suggests that boys and girls are treated differently in each of the six areas listed below. Write a brief sentence for each area recalling your experiences. Do you agree or disagree with assumption? Based on the statements would you say your gender role training was typical or atypical? Write a brief paragraph about your gender role training.

Parents rewarding:

Aggression

Independence

Boisterousness

Nurturance

Affectiveness

Compliance

The Contemporary

6.   A *nuclear* family (as opposed to an *extended* family) consists of mother, father, and children, and is no longer the most common North American family. Baumrind describes parenting styles as permissive (nonpunitive, noncontrolling, nondemanding), authoritarian (dogmatic, controlling, obedience-oriented), or authoritative (firm but based on reason, nondogmatic, geared toward promoting independence but encouraging adherence to standards)-- and advocates authoritative parenting. Both the psychoanalytic and the behavioristic models probably exaggerate the extent to which the child is susceptible to external influences. Three important sources of childcare advice are the medical profession, books, and parenting courses.

Exercise 6:   Listed below is a checklist of behaviors reflecting each family style. Based on this checklist, which parenting style do you believe was most dominant in your family? Based on the information in the chapter and your personality do you agree? Write a brief paragraph on the style you feel was most predominant in your family.

Family Composition

7.   Firstborn and only children often have some achievement and intellectual advantages over their siblings--as do children whose siblings are much younger or older than they are. Children from larger families sometimes do less well than children from smaller families on measures of intellectual performance. These observations are due mainly to the social and economic characteristics of large and small families, and to the influence of birth order, birth interval, and family size on the relationships most likely to develop between children and their parents.

Exercise 7a: List 3 first born children you know (this may include yourself). Would you say the hypothesis about higher intelligence and academic achievement is true?

Exercise 7b.   List 3 friends you know from larger families (this may include yourself). Would you say the hypothesis about low intelligence is true?

Exercise 7c: List 3 people you know whose age interval i.e., siblings are significantly younger or older (this may include yourself). Would you say this hypothesis about their being more creative is true?

Based on all of the above do you personally believe there is a relationship between family composition and those characteristics listed in the book? Do you have any observations of your own based on your observations?

One-Parent Families

8.   Some of the possible negative effects of divorce and separation on children relate to the child's age: Preschool children may view divorce as a parent leaving them because they have been "bad"; older children may experience anger and hostility, mixed with sadness; adolescents may view the situation more realistically. These effects may be due to absence of a parent, family conflict, economic hardship, and stressful life changes, and are more serious with greater parental *disengagement.* An increasing number of more recent studies find few long-term negative effects of divorce, perhaps because now it is more common and more socially accepted.

Exercise 8:   If possible list 3 to 5 people you know who are from divorced or separated families and parents have remarried. Based on your knowledge about them would you say they show, or have shown any adverse effects of the divorce? Do they still talk about it or discuss it in anyway? Do you think it influences this relationship with others -- particularly the opposite sex (you may be one of these people)? Has it influenced you?

Exercise 8b: List all of the people you know who are one parent families as a result of divorce or separation. Do you observe adverse effects as a result of the divorce or separation? Do you think that it influences their relationships with others -- particularly the opposite sex? (You may be one of these people. Has it influenced you?)

Based on this simple observation above do you believe divorce or separation has long range detrimental effects on children?

Children in Stepfamilies

9. Stepfamilies result from the remarriage of a widowed or divorced parent. Stepchildren sometimes face problems relating to loss of some of the parent's time and affection, establishing relationships with stepfamily members, and abandoning the fantasy that the biological parents may reunite. In many cases, these potential problems are insignificant or nonexistent.

Exercise 9: Consider yourself a marriage counselor and your client Sasha, a mother of two children (Allen 9, Sarah 3) is considering remarriage. consider the possible problems as well as the positive side of her decision. What points would you make with her in discussing the pros and cons taking into account the benefits to her and her would-be-husband, the children and the relatives on both sides.

Nonparental Child Care

10. Nonparental child care does not generally have negative effects on the social, emotional, or cognitive development of children and can, in fact, have beneficial effects, especially for children from disadvantaged homes. Important factors to consider when selecting a day-care facility include staff-children ratio, physical environment, equipment and materials provided for children, financial resources, and the qualifications of staff members.

Exercise 10: Beth and Clem are looking for a good child care program. They seek your advice being the expert on lifespan development. What would you tell them to look for in making a decision?

I.   Reading and Understanding

**Physical and Cognitive Development: Middle Childhood
Chapter 9**

This Chapter
        Middle Childhood
Physical and Motor Development
--Height and Weight
        --Fat and Fat-Free Mass
                --lean body mass
                --white adipose tissue
        --The Growth Spurt
                --average
                --peak height velocity
--Nutrition and Health
        --Obesity
        --Diseases and Infections
--Motor Development
        --Sex Differences in Motor Performance
        --Explanations of Sex Differences
--Physical Fitness
        --performance
        --health-related
--Some Physical and Sensory Problems
        --exceptional
        --Visual Impairment
                --mainstreaming
        --Hearing Impairment
                --hard of hearing
                --prelinguistic
                --postlinguistic
                --otitis media
                --p-b, t-d, and f-v
        --Other Problems
--The Physically Gifted
Intellectual Development: Piaget's View
        --concrete operation
--The Conservations
        --quantities
        --conserve
        --Constructing Knowledge
                --meaning-making
                --constructing knowledge
                --operations
                --preoperations
                --field effects
        --Rules of Logic
                --identity
                --reversibility
                --compensation
--Acceleration of Conservation
--Seriation, Number, and Classes
        --Classes
        --Series
                --seriation

--Number
    --ordinal
    --cardinal
--A Summary of Concrete Operations
    --operation
    --operational
The Child As Information Processor
    --information-processing approach
    --knowledge base
    --cognitive strategies
        --game of cognition
    --metacognition
        --knowing about knowing
--Components of Memory
    --working memory
    --processing
--Sensory Memory
--Short-Term Memory
    --working
    --chunking
    --rehearsal
--Long-Term memory
    --generative
    --scripts
    --understanding
--Types of Long-Term Memory
    --Declarative Versus Nondeclarative Memory
        --nondeclarative memory
        --implicit memory
        --declarative memory
        --explicit memory
            --conscious
            --unconscious
    --Semantic Versus Episodic Memory
        --general knowledge
        --semantic memory
            --personal memories
        --episodic memory
            --autobiographical
--Processes in Long-Term Memory
    --Rehearsing
    --Elaborating
    --Organizing
--Developmental Changes in Memory
    --Sensory and Short-Term memory
    --Longer-Term Memory
    --Children as Witnesses
--Metacognition and Metamemory
--Teaching Strategies
    --Socratic dialogue
    --cognitive apprenticeship
--A Summary of Memory Development
    --game of cognition

Intelligence
--What Is Intelligence?
    --general factor theory
    --special abilities theory
    --Fluid and Crystallized Abilities
        --fluid abilities (or fluid intelligence)
    --A Contextual Approach
        --contextual theory of intelligence
        --metacomponents
        --performance components
        --knowledge-acquisition components
--Measuring Intelligence
    --individual intelligence tests
    --group intelligence tests
        --WAIS-R (Wechsler Adult Intelligence Scale Revised
        --Wechsler Preschool and Primary Scale of Intelligence
--Developmental Changes in IQ
    --psychometrically
    --compared
--Misconceptions and Facts About IQ
    --Misconception 1
        --IQ is a mysterious something possessed in lesser or greater quantities by
            everyone
    --Misconception 2
        --IQ is a constant. I have x amount, you have y, and that's that
    --Misconception 3
        --IQ tests are fair measures of all the important things
    --Misconception 4
        --IQ tests are fair
            --culture fair
    --Fact
        --IQ is related to academic and job success
Intellectual Exceptionality
--Mental Retardation
    --Definition
    --general intellectual functioning
    --impairments in adaptive behavior
    --manifested during the developmental period
    --Identification
    --Prevalence
    --Causes
        --organic
        --familial
        --pre or postnatal
    --Categories and Characteristics
        --mild
        --moderate
        --severe
        --profound
        --educable
        --trainable
        --custodial
        --mildly retarded
        --educable mentally retarded (EMR)
        --moderately retarded
        --mainstreamed
        --mental retardation
        --profoundly mentally retarded

--Learning Disabilities
    --hyperactivity
    --learning dysfunction
    --cerebral dysfunction
    --minimal brain damage
    --perceptual handicaps
    --dyslexia
    --perceptual disability
    --slow learners
    --brain damage or cerebral dysfunction
    --Definition
        --learning disability
    --Symptoms and identification
    --Categories
    --developmental reading disorder
        --dyslexia
        --specific reading disability
    --developmental arithmetic disorder
        process disorders
--Intellectual Giftedness
--Creativity and Giftedness
    --Identifying the Gifted and Creative
        --personality inventories
        --biographical and activity inventories
        --behavioral measures
        --divergent thinking
        --convergent thinking
        --fluency
        --flexibility
        --originality
        --class
    --Some Characteristics of Creative and Gifted Children
        --academic self-concept
        --game of cognition
        --metacognitive skills
    --A Context for Eminence
        --parents
--Trends and controversies in Special Education
    --Mainstreaming
        --adaptive education
    --Labeling
The Magical Child

II. Learning and Comprehending
Scrambles
Chapter 9

Scramble 1
Now that you are an expert on Piaget's Stages of Cognitive Development just rattle off the stage, approximate age and 3 major characteristics of that stage in correct sequence.

Stage	Approximate Age	Three Major Characteristics	Points
_____	_____	_____ _____ _____	_____
_____	_____	_____ _____ _____	_____
_____	_____	_____ _____ _____	_____

Your Total Points _____
Total Possible Points _____
Total Points   15

1. World of the here and now
2. Sensorimotor
3. 7 to 11-12 years
4. Development of reversibility in thought
5. Ability to deal with the hypothetical
6. No notion of objective reality
7. Understanding of number
8. 11-12 to 14-15 years
9. 0-2 years
10. Motoric intelligence
11. Ability to conserve
12. Concrete operations
13. Propositional thinking
14. Development of strong idealism
15. Formal operations

Scramble 2.
Rattle off the 2 Substages of the Preoperational stage and give one major characteristic (in correct age sequence).

Preoperational	Approximate Age	One Major Characteristic	Points
_____	_____	_____	_____
_____	_____	_____	_____
	_____	_____	_____

Your Total Points _____
Total Possible Points _____
Total Points   8

1. Intuitive
2. 2-7 years
3. Reason dominated by perception
4. Preconceptual
5. Intuitive rather than logical solutions
6. 4-7 years
7. Egocentric thought
8. 2-4 years

Scramble 3:

Listed below are the 3 levels of memory along with descriptive categories. Match the description with the level of memory.

Description	Sensory	Short Term	Long Term	Points
Alternate labels	_____	_____	_____	_____
Deviation	_____	_____	_____	_____
Stability	_____	_____	_____	_____
Capacity	_____	_____	_____	_____
General Characteristics	_____	_____	_____	_____

Your Total Points	_____	
Total Possible Points	_____	
Total Points	15	

1. Immediate consciousness
2. Indefinite
3. Echoic or iconic
4. Primary or working
5. Fleeting
6. Easily disrupted
7. Unlimited
8. Associationistic
9. Less than 20 seconds
10. Limited
11. Secondary
12. Momentary, unconscious impression
13. Limited (7 ± 2 items)
14. Less than 1 second
15. Not easily disrupted

Scramble 4:   **Listed below is a mixture of verbal and performance scales from the WISC. Place the appropriate sub scale under the appropriate category.**

Verbal Scale   **Performance Scale**   **Points**

_____   _____   _____   _____   _____

_____   _____   _____   _____   _____

_____   _____   _____   _____   _____

                                    _____

                                                    Your Total Points   _____
                                                    Total Possible Points   _____
                                                    Total Points   13

1.   Coding
2.   Arithmetic
3.   Similarities
4.   Digit Span
5.   Picture Completion
6.   Block Design
7.   General Information
8.   Mazes
9.   Symbol Search
10. Vocabulary
11. Picture Arrangement
12. General Comprehension
13. Object Assembly

Scramble Summary

		Points
Scramble 1	**Piaget's Stages of Cognitive Development**	_____
Scramble 2	**Substages of Preoperational Stage**	_____
Scramble 3	**Levels of Memory**	_____
Scramble 4	**WISC Subscales**	_____

                                    Your Total Points   _____
                                    Total Possible Points 51
                                    % =   _____

III.   Experiencing

Main Points and Exercises

Exercises
Chapter 9

Physical and Motor Development

1.   Boys are normally heavier and taller than girls throughout life, but the female growth spurt occurs earlier. Girls retain a higher percentage of fat mass than do boys throughout life. Obesity (linked to overeating, underexercising, and genetic background) is the most common childhood nutritional problem in North America. Children are more fit than is generally thought.

Exercise 1A: You and your friend, Zeke are watching kids on the playground. Zeke comments on how weird the group is -- tall, short, skinny and fat. Being now an expert on lifespan development, straighten out Zeke on what you have learned about individual height and weight differences on children in middle childhood.

Exercise 1B: Wilma and Fred are worried about their 8 year old Pebbles being so small compared to the other children her age. Be the reassuring friend and let them know about height and weight at this age. (You can also apply this idea in case other friends talk about the embarrassment of their child being too tall).

2.   The majority of children classified legally blind (corrected vision poorer than 2/200 in the better eye) can see well enough to read large print and to function normally in society. Hearing impairments (often congenital or associated with otitis media) have more social-emotional and academic problems associated with them, largely because of language deficits.

Exercise 2A: Clem does not understand the vision thing about 20/20, 20/200, etc. Now that you have read about it explain it to him. Although it is not in the book explain 4/20 or exceptional vision?

Exercise 2B: Want to know what it's like to be deaf? Turn the sound off while you are watching TV and try to lip read. Can you pick up the general area of information? Do you notice focusing a little more on the mouth? lips? What cues do you use? Do you notice the difficulty of distinguishing p from b? t from d? from v? any other problems?

Intellectual Development: Piaget's View

3.   *Conservation* is the realization that certain transformations do not change the quantitative features of objects, and may reflect the logic rules of *identity, reversibility,* and *compensation.* Attempts to accelerate the acquisition of specific conservations have met with mixed success. In addition to the conservations, children acquire abilities relating classification, seriation, and number.

Exercise 3:   Explain to Guy and Francine why their child, Fedrick thinks there is more water in a tall glass than there is in a much wider glass, even though there is the same amount in each. Here is your big chance to show off your knowledge about this conservation especially the logic rules of identity, reversibility and compensation.

The Child as Information Processor

4.   Information-processing approaches to cognition look at knowledge base, strategies for dealing with cognitive material, and awareness of the self as a knower or as a processor of information. Memory (closely related to knowledge base and to cognitive strategies) may be described in terms of three components; sensory memory (the momentary effect of sense impressions), short-term memory (similar to attention span; seconds long, highly limited), and long-term memory (indefinite duration; requires cognitive processing). Long-term memory may be declarative (explicit, verbalizable) or nondeclarative (implicit, nonverbalizable). Declarative memory may be semantic (stable, abstract knowledge base) or episodic (memory for personal events). The three basic memory processes are rehearsal (repetition), elaboration (extending or adding something to material), and organization (forming associations).

Exercise 4A: Two of your friends, Cid and Cy are in an argument about memory. Both are way off base. Your expertise, gained from your knowledge in the Lifespan Development class enables you to tell them about the three components of memory - sensory, short-term and long-term. How would you describe these three components to them?

Exercise 4B: Cid and Cy are impressed by your knowledge and want to know how you remember so much. Here is your chance to tell them about types of long-term memory and the three basic memory processes involved. This exercise will not only help them but will help to reinforce your long-term memory.

5.   Sensory and short-term memory, which are not highly dependent on strategies, are not very different in younger and older children, but long-term memory is superior in detail in older children and adults. However, both make about the same proportion of errors in "witness" studies. Developmental changes in long-term memory may be due to the development of processing abilities in children and to their eventual recognition of their own cognitive processes (metacognition and metamemory).

Exercise 5:   As a final note to the two friends you have been talking to (Cid and Cy) you might just tell them about the developmental changes in long-term memory (from children to adults) They will be truly impressed when you define metacognition and metamemory.

Intelligence

6.   Some describe intelligence as a general factor underlying ability that determines performance in all areas; some describe it in terms of separate and distinct abilities. Cattell describes *fluid abilities* (unlearned, unaffected by culture, evident in the ability to solve abstract problems and to reason) and *crystallized abilities* (learned, highly influenced by culture, reflected in measures of vocabulary and general information). Sternberg's *contextual* theory defines intelligence in terms of how well people adapt and function in context. His three components of intelligence are *metacomponents* (metacognition and metamemory, executive functions), *performance components* (intellectual skills such as analyzing, sorting, elaborating), and the *knowledge-acquisition component* (what is achieved in the process of learning).

Exercise 6:   Parents are often sensitive to and concerned about their children's intelligence. If you were drawn into a conversation and asked about intelligence how would you define it? As a Lifespan Development study you may wish to explain Cattell's approach describing fluid and crystallized abilities. Or you may elaborate on Sternberg's contextual theory including the metacomponents, performance components and the knowledge-acquisition component. Or you may wish to describe to the parents BOTH theories which would have them thinking YOU ARE REALLY INTELLIGENT.

7.   Two widely used individual (one child at a time) intelligence tests are the Stanford-Binet and the Wechsler tests. Defined psychometrically, average IQ does not change from year to year; however, the measured intelligence of any given individual before the age of 2 does not predict later intelligence as well as tests given later. Measured IQ is not a mystical, fixed, unchanging, and unmodifiable something. Intelligence tests often do not measure a variety of important things (interpersonal skills, motivation, creativity, athletic and musical ability) and are often culturally biased.

Exercise 7A: Do you know your IQ score? How does it make you feel? Have you changed your attitude about that score as a result of what you have learned in the text? Imagine yourself explaining an IQ score to someone who did not understand the concept. In addition describe the IQ tests, how they are developed and how they relate to school performance to this same person.

Exercise 7B: The four misperceptions of IQ are listed below. Without referring back to the text how would you combat each statement if you were put in a position to do so?

Misperception 1.   IQ is a mysterious something in lesser or greater quantities by everyone.
Misperception 2:   IQ is a constant. I have x amount, you have Y, and that's that.
Misperception 3:   IQ tests are fair measures of all important things.
Misperception 4:   IQ tests are fair.

Exercise 7C: How would you combat the statement "IQ tests are a joke. They aren't related to anything. It's just a way of separating people and they don't mean anything."

Intellectual Exceptionality

8. Mental retardation is characterized by a general depression in the ability to learn and is defined in low measured intelligence and poor childhood adaptation. It is currently classified in terms of the severity of retardation, regardless of cause (mild, moderate, severe, and profound). Learning disabilities include a wide range of specific learning problems not associated with mental retardation or other physical or emotional disturbances (performance below expectation). They are often manifested in language-related problems and are often evident in difficulties associated with learning to read or to do arithmetic (developmental reading disorder -- *dyslexia*-- and developmental arithmetic disorder).

Exercise 8A: You are a school psychologist who has just finished testing a child and the results indicate that the child is functioning at a mild level of retardation. Assuming that these results are highly reliable how would you describe the results to the parents?

Exercise 8B: Minnie's child has dyslexia but she does not know the difference between that and retardation. How would you explain the difference so she may be reassured?

9. Intellectual giftedness is manifested in exceptional intelligence, exceptional creativity, and high motivation. Creativity is often defined in terms of innovation or originality and may involve intellectual characteristics not ordinarily measured by intelligence tests. The family context is extremely important in the development of eminence.

Exercise 9: Now that you know creativity is a combination of fluency, flexibility and originality lets push your creative potential. Listed below are 3 items. Without outside help see if you can come up with 30 responses for each one. Of the 30 make 10 very flexible and 10 very original. Ready -- here they are: sea cucumber, saliva, and a blade of grass. Good luck!

10. Recent trends in special education include deinstitutionalization, mainstreaming, and an antilabeling movement. Each is characterized by some controversy.

Exercise 10. Let's play the labeling game. Listed below are descriptions of intelligence, creativity and motivation.

5. Extremely intelligent	5. Extremely Creative	5. Extremely Motivated
4. Above Average Intelligence	4. Above Average in Creativity	4. Above Average in Motivation
3. Average Intelligence	3. Average Creativity	3. Average Motivation
2. Slightly Below Average in Intelligence	2. Slightly Below Average in Creativity	2. Slightly Below Average in Motivation
1. Low Intelligence	1. Low Creativity	1. Low Motivation

For each trait, intelligence, creativity and motivation select where you think you rank. (You don't have to mark the sheet if you feel sensitive just on an additional sheet of paper.) Now put the numbers in sequence. For example if you were 4 on intelligence, a 3 on creativity and a 5 on motivation you could refer to yourself as 4-3-5 . Now give that combination of numbers a label -- of your own making. How do you feel being that label? What if people referred to the numbers without knowing you? Take a few moments to think of what that number label means and how others who have labels must feel.

I.   Reading and Understanding

Social Development: Middle Childhood
Chapter 10

This Chapter
Social Cognition
--The Origins of Social Cognition
--Theories of Mind
        --Role Taking and Empathy
Self-Worth
--self-concept
--self-worth
--self-esteem
--Some Definitions
        --self-concept
        --positive
        --negative
        --self-esteem
        --self-worth
        --self-appraisal
--Two Approaches to Self-Worth
        --James's Approach
        --Cooley's Approach
--Measuring Self-Worth
--Some Investigations of Self-Worth
        --Some Important Findings
                --scholastic competence
                --athletic competence
                --social acceptance
                --physical appearance
                --behavioral conduct
        --Some Implications
Friends and Peers
--Children's Views of Friendship
--Dimensions of Childhood Friendships
        --Best Friends
        --Sex Differences
        --Importance of Friends
--Peer Groups
--Parents and Peers
--Peer Acceptance
        --sociometric status
                --peer ratings
                --peer nominations
--Sociometric Status
        --social isolates
        --Five Levels of social Status
                --Sociometric stars
                --Teacher negatives
                --sociometric rejectees
        --Qualities Related to Peer Acceptance
                --status
        --Qualities Related to Peer Rejection
--Consequences of Peer Acceptance and Rejection
        --sociability

The School
--Schooling and Measured Intelligence
--Teacher Expectations
         --self-fulfilling prophecies
         --The Self-Fulfilling Prophecy
--Attribution Theory
         --attribution
         --mastery-oriented
         --learned helplessness
         --How Mastery-Oriented and Helpless Children Differ
Television
--viewing Patterns
--Comprehension
--Does Television Viewing Lead to Aggression and Violence?
         --aggression
         --violence
         --Laboratory Research on the Effects of Television Violence
         --Naturalistic Research on the Effects of Television Violence
         --Cross-Cultural Comparisons
                 --Surgeon General's Report on Television and Social Behavior
--Other Possible Negative Effects of Television
         --fear
--Positive Effects of Television
--Why Is Television Influential?
         --imitation
         --attitude-change
         --information-processing
         --scripts
--Rock Videos, VCRs, and Video Games
         --Rock Videos
         --VCRs
         --Video Games
--A Summary of the Television Controversy
Violence in the Family
--Prevalence of Child Maltreatment
--Nature of Child Maltreatment
         --Physical Abuse
         --Physical Neglect
         --Emotional Abuse
         --Sexual Abuse
--The Consequences of Maltreatment
         --General Effects of Maltreatment
         --Possible Effects of Sexual Abuse
--The Abusive Family Context
         --Characteristics of Abusive Parents
         --Who Is Maltreated?
--What Can Be done?
Social-Emotional Exceptionality
--Prevalence, Classifications, and Contributing factors
         --Classifications
         --Contributing Factors
         --Risk and Resilience
--Attention Deficit Hyperactivity Disorder (ADHD)
         --Diagnosis
         --Treatment
         --Causes
--Other Behavior Disorders

--Stress in Childhood
      --Stress Defined
      --The Effects of Stress
            --threat
            --challenge
      --Stress in Childhood
            --stimulus
            --demand
            --responsibility overload
            --change overload
            --emotional overload
            --information overload
            --hurried child
--Social-Emotional Giftedness

Scrambles
Chapter 10

Scramble 1   **Selman's Developmental Progression In Social Cognition**

Perspective-Taking Stage	Age	Description	Points
0 _____	0-6	_____	_____
1 _____	6-8	_____	_____
2 _____	8-10	_____	_____
3 _____	10-12	_____	_____
4 _____	12-15+	_____	_____

Your Total Points   _____
Total Possible Points   10
% =   _____

1.   Self-reflective (8-10)
2.   "There is no perspective but mine. People feel the way I would in that situation."
3.   Social and conventional
4.   "Actually, we can have different points of view. There's hers and there's mine. I can see mine; she can see hers:"
5.   Egocentric (to 6 years)
6.   "Actually, within the context of discombobulism, and taking into consideration the teachings of..."
7.   Mutual (10-12)
8.   "Okay, so others have a point of view too, but they would feel the way I do if they had the same information."
9.   Social-informational (6-8)
10.   "Well, maybe I can see hers and she can see mine. We can even talk about our different points of view."

Scramble 2:   **Match the Five Categories of Social Status with Appropriate Characteristics.**

Category	Characteristics	Points
_____	_____	_____
_____	_____	_____
_____	_____	_____
_____	_____	_____
_____	_____	_____

Your Total Points	_____
Total Possible Points	10
% =	_____

1. Especially well liked by most
2. Tuned out
3. Not involved; are ignored rather than rejected
4. Sociometric stars
5. High peer interaction. Some well liked; others not
6. Sociometric rejectees
7. Not liked very much. Rejected rather than simply ignored
8. Teacher negatives
9. Typically in conflict with teachers. Some are liked; others not
10. Mixers

Scramble Summary

		Points
Scramble 1	**Selman's Developmental Progression**	_____
Scramble 2	**Five Categories of Social Status**	_____

Your Total Points	_____
Total Possible Points	20
% =	_____

III. Experiencing

Main Points and Exercises

Exercises
Chapter 10

Social Cognition

1. *Social cognition* refers to an awareness of ourselves and of others as being capable of feelings, motives, intentions, and so on. Its development implies that the child has begun to develop a theory of mind. Selman's five stages of role taking reflect the child's ability to verbalize other perspectives; *egocentric* (to age 6; one point of view), *social-informational* (6-8; my view is correct, others less informed), *self-reflective* (8-10; people are aware only of their views), *mutual* (10-12; people recognize and talk about each other's views), and *social and conventional* (12-15+; abstract recognition of different views).

Exercise 1:   Your neighbor, Tim, doesn't understand why his son Jason, age 4 doesn't act like his brother Mick, age 12 when it comes to understanding how others feel. Explain to him, Selman's developmental progression in social cognition and the various stages of development.

Self-worth

2. *Self-worth* refers to personal evaluations of the self. James viewed self-worth in terms of the discrepancy between the real individual and aspirations; Cooley argued that self-worth reflects how we think others evaluate us. After age 8, children can make global assessments of self-worth and separate evaluations in five areas; scholastic, athletic, physical appearance, social acceptance, and morality. The most important sources of information in determining the child's self-worth stem from parents and classmates (rather than from friends or teachers). High self-wroth is associated with happiness; low self-worth, with sadness and depression. In turn, these moods are linked with motivation.

Exercise 2:   Ted and Tina want a child who has feelings of being worthwhile. Give them a two minute lecture on James and Cooley's theories, what their role as parents may be and what they can do.

Friends and Peers

3.   For preschoolers, friendship is playing together; in middle childhood, friendships involve enduring, reciprocal relationships. Most children have more than one "best" friend. Friends and peers are critical for positive self-concepts and for learning sex-appropriate values and attitudes.

Exercise 3:   You have a class project that involves determining the popularity of the students in a fifth grade class. Outline how you would use peer ratings or peer nominations in developing a sociogram.

4.   Social competence contributes to high status; social incompetence contributes to lower status. Five categories of social status determined through sociometry are: *sociometric stars* (especially well liked), *mixers* (high interaction, *teacher negatives* (conflict with teachers), *tuned out*) uninvolved; ignored rather than rejected), and *sociometric rejectees* (not liked). High social competence is reflected in the child's ability to sense what is happening in social groups, in a high degree of responsiveness to others, and in an understanding that relationships develop slowly over time.

Exercise 4:   Listed below are the 5 categories of social status. Personally review your days in grade school and put a classmate beside each category. Finally, where would you fall?

> Sociometric Star
> Mixer
> Teacher Negative
> Tuned Out
> Sociometric Rejectees

The School

5.   The school is a powerful socializing and intellectual influence. Teacher expectations may affect student performance, as might the student's tendency to be *mastery-oriented* (accepting personal responsibility for outcomes, attributing them to intelligence or effort, for example) or *helpless* (accepting no responsibility, attributing outcomes to things like luck or task difficulty).

Exercise 5A: Circle the statement, or phrase which best describes you.

It is important for me to be successful - Success isn't that important to me.
I create my own luck - Luck happens to me.
I enjoy a challenging task - I usually avoid challenging tasks.
I expect to do well in this class - I don't think I'll do well in this class.
I make things happen - Things happen to me.

The above quiz is obviously a crude form of the internal vs. external control scale. If you have been honest and marked everything on the left you are internally controlled. If you have marked all or some of the things on the right you are externally controlled. Rereading the material on mastery-oriented and helplessness may be valuable in rethinking self perception.

Exercise 5B: What would be the steps you would take to insure that your child would become a mastery oriented student. Make an outline you feel you could confidently share with others in helping them with their child.

Television

6.   Young children spend approximately one third of their waking hours watching television, but do not comprehend all they see. There is evidence of a relationship between television viewing and aggression. Pro-social television themes can have positive effects. An information-processing explanation for the effects of television maintains that children encode violence (represent it mentally), rehearse and elaborate it in fantasy (the result of seeing variations of it in different television programs), and then retrieve it along with relevant scripts (routines detailing the sequence in which the violence is to be perpetrated) when they are moved to aggression.

Exercise 6A: Make a review of your personal television viewing. List your favorite programs or the programs you have watched the most in the past week. For each program (or each show, list the main theme, i.e., adventure, sex, violence, humor, etc.) Now write a simple paragraph relating how TV has either influenced your decision making for the week in a positive or negative way.

Exercise 6B: Your close friend Tabatha has a child starting in the first grade and wants your expert opinion on a TV viewing policy for her child during the school year. Outline what you would tell her and why.

Violence in the Family

7.   Violence touches many North American homes each year, some of it in the form of child abuse which may be *physical abuse* (punching, kicking, beating), *physical neglect* (failure to provide food, clothing, shelter, health care), *emotional abuse* (habitual ridicule, scolding, ostracism), or *sexual abuse* (sexual behaviors forced upon the child). Any of these forms of abuse can have serious and long-lasting physical and psychological consequences. Many infants are included among abused children (more probable if the infant is premature, deformed, or irritable, or if the other is overworked, often pregnant, or depressed) Nonwhites are overrepresented among this group in the United States. The abusive family context may include abusers who are disturbed in a clinical sense (although often they are not); individuals who were themselves abused when young restrictive, authoritarian parenting; and parental emotional unavailability. It is difficult to predict who is most likely to be abused or who is most likely to abuse. Some programs for preventing child abuse and treating its consequences suggest changing attitudes toward the use of physical punishment.

Exercise 7:   You have been asked to give a 5 minute talk on abuse to a group of new parents. Briefly outline what you would say about each of the 4 areas of abuse and give an example.

Social-Emotional Exceptionality

8.   The causes of emotional disorders include predisposing factors (genetics and environmental conditions, such as parental abuse) and precipitating factors (specific environmental events, such as the death of a parent or serious illness) Knowledge of a child's biological and environmental history sometimes makes it possible to identify those who run a higher risk of emotional disturbance.

Exercise 8:   Describe to Anita and Andy the causes of emotional disorders including genetic and environmental conditions as well as precipitating factors. Explain how some children run a higher risk than others.

9.   *Attention deficit hyperactivity disorder* (ADHD, often simply called *hyperactivity*) is characterized by excessive activity and deficits in attention span without evidence of brain damage or neurological dysfunction. Hyperactive children frequently present behavior problems for teachers and are sometimes treated with stimulant drugs. Other behavior disorders are manifested in socialization problems; extreme defiance (*oppositional defiance disorder*); misbehaviors such as lying, stealing, delinquency, and aggression; social withdrawal and excessive shyness; and eating disorders.

Exercise 9:   Ben and Sara have a very active child. Using the criteria on table 10.8 how would you differentiate between the "normal" child and an ADHD child.

10.   Stress among children can result from many sources including fears, responsibility overload, change overload, emotional overload, school-related stress, and information overload. Scales that look at major events in children's lives are sometimes useful in identifying the possibility of stress-related problems. Some children are more resistant to stress (*resilient*) than others.

Exercise 10:   You have been asked to address a group of pre-school mothers on the topic of the "hurried child". What would be your outline and what SPECIFICS would you recommend to avoid the problem.

I.   **Reading and Understanding**

Physical and Cognitive Development: Adolescence
Chapter 11

This Chapter
Adolescence as Transition
--Primitive Transitions
        --rites of passage
        --taboo
        --initiation
        --induction
--Contemporary Transitions and Rites
        --discontinuous societies
        --continuous societies
        --sturm and drang
                --rites de passage
                --separation
                --training
                --initiation and induction
Physical and Biological
        --Puberty
        --Pubescence
--Physical Changes
        --Height and Weight
        --Body Composition
        --Strength and Motor Performance
--Pubescence: Sexual Changes
        --Pubescence
                --primary sexual characteristics
                --ovaries
                --testes
                --secondary sexual characteristics
--Puberty: Sexual Maturity
        --Menarche
        --Age of Puberty
--Early and Late Maturation
        --Effects for Boys
        --Effects for Girls
        --An Ecological Interpretation
--Some Concerns of Adolescents
Nutrition and Eating Disorders
--Obesity
        --thinness
--Anorexia nervosa
        --Definition
        --Prevalence
        --Causes
--Bulimia Nervosa
        --Definition
        --Prevalence
        --Causes
        --Some Treatments
                --behavior therapy
                --rational
                --group
                --individual

Adolescent Intellectual Development
      --assimilating
      --accommodating
      --equilibrating
--Piaget's View: Formal Operations
      --A Piagetian Problem
      --Formal Versus Concrete Thinking
            --imagining
            --concrete
            --hypothetical
            --logical
            --logic of propositions
      --Implications of Formal Thinking
--An Information-Processing View
      --Changes in Knowledge Base
      --Changes in Processing
      --Metacognitive Change
Adolescent Egocentrism
      --egocentrism
      --selfishness
      --self-centeredness
      --imaginary audience
--The Imaginary Audience
      --Measuring the Imaginary Audience
            --Imaginary Audience Scale (IAS)
            --Adolescent Egocentrism-Sociocentrism Scale
      --Implications of the Imaginary Audience
--The Personal Fable
--Reckless Adolescent Behavior
      --Manifestations of Adolescent Recklessness
      --Why Adolescents Take Risks
--The Cautious Adolescent
Moral Development
      --Morality
--Morality as A Cognitive Phenomenon
--Piaget's Approach
      --Piaget's Two Stages of Moral Development
            --heteronomy
--Kohlberg's Stages
      --Preconventional
            --preconventional level
            --hedonistic
      --Conventional
      --Postconventional
      --A Seventh Stage?
--Research on the Views of Piaget and Kohlberg
--More Recent Findings and Conclusions
--Gilligan's Approach: Gender Differences
      --Female Morality
      --Gilligan's View of Male-Female Differences
            --caring
            --abstract justice
      --Other Research on Male-Female Differences
            --in a different voice
--Implications of Research on Moral Development
      --School Influences
      --Family Influences

II. Learning and Comprehending

Scrambles
Chapter 11

Scramble 1:   Listed below are physiological events for the normal sequence of sexual motivation for North American Boys and girls. Match the sequence with the appropriate physiological event

Sequence Boys	Physiological Events	Sequence Girls	Physiological Events	Points
1.	_____	1.	_____	_____
2.	_____	2.	_____	_____
3.	_____	3.	_____	_____
4.	_____	4.	_____	_____
5.	_____	5.	_____	_____
6.	_____	6.	_____	_____
7.	_____	7.	_____	_____
8.	_____	8.	_____	_____
9.	_____	9.	_____	_____
10.	_____	10.	_____	_____

Your Total Points   _____
Total Possible Points   19
% =   _____

1. Beginning of adolescent growth spurt
2. Enlargement of penis
3. Appearance of unpigmented pubic down; growth of testes and scrotum (sac containing testes)
4. Development of axillary (armpit) hair; continued enlargement of breasts; slight lowering of the voice
5. Increase in size of vagina, clitoris, and uterus
6. Appearance of pigmented, kinky pubic hair
7. Development of axillary (armpit) hair; growth of facial hair
8. Growth of chest hair
9. Appearance of unpigmented public down
10. Lowering of voice; appearance of "down" on upper lip
11. Menarche
12. Decline in rate of physical growth
13. Increase in production of oil; increased perspiration; possible acne
14. First ejaculations occur
15. Breast elevation ("bud" stage)

Scramble 2:   **Rank the adolescent concerns listed below from 1 to 12.**

Rank	Concerns	Points
1.	_____	_____
2.	_____	_____
3.	_____	_____
4.	_____	_____
5.	_____	_____
6.	_____	_____
7.	_____	_____
8.	_____	_____
9.	_____	_____
10.	_____	_____
11.	_____	_____
12.	_____	_____

Your Total Points _____
Total Possible Points   12
% =   _____

1. Time (not enough time to do the things they want)
2. Feelings of inferiority (poor self-image)
3. What am I going to do when I finish school?
4. Finances (40 percent of respondents worked part-time)
5. Parents' marriage
6. Boredom
7. Appearance
8. School concerns
9. What is the purpose of life?
10. Height or weight
11. Sex
12. Loneliness

Scramble 3: There are 18 possible medical consequences of bulimia nervosa. After reading the consequences on Table 11.4 see if you can remember 10.

1. _____   6. _____

2. _____   7. _____

3. _____   8. _____

4. _____   9. _____

5. _____   10. _____

Your Total Points   _____
Total Possible Points   10
% =   _____

Scramble 4:   **Fill in the Components of Moral Behavior**

Moral Behavior Requires	Possible Reasons for Not Intervening	Points
Moral sensitivity (recognition of a moral problem)	1. **Individual's values run counter to helping someone in this situation**	_____
Moral judgment (deciding what *ought* to be done)	2. **Inability to devise a plan of behavior compatible with ideals and values ("How can I save her without endangering mine?")**	_____
Moral values (conscience; ideals; that which guides moral action)	3. **Unable to implement the plan the individual might have devised ("I should restrain the attacker physically, but I'm not strong enough.")**	_____
Moral action (implementing moral or immoral behavior)	4. **Failure to recognize seriousness of situation ("It's only a lover's quarrel.")**	_____

Your Total Points   _____
Total Possible Points   4
% =   _____

Scramble 5:   **Fill in the Kohlberg's Levels of Morality.**

Level I Preconventional   **Stage 1**   _____   _____
                                                 Stage 2   _____   _____

Level II   Conventional   **Stage 3**   _____   _____
                                                      Stage 4.   _____   _____

Level III   Postconventional   **Stage 5.**   _____   _____
                                                            Stage 6.   _____   _____
                                                            Stage 7.   _____   _____

Your Total Points   _____
Total Possible Points   7
% =   _____

1.   Naive instrumental hedonism
2.   Law-and-order orientation
3.   Universal ethical
4.   "Good-boy, nice-girl" morality
5.   Punishment and obedience orientation
6.   Morality of social contract
7.   Religious, metaphorical

Scramble Summary

		Your Points
Scramble 1:	**Physiological Events**	_____
Scramble 2:	**Rank of Adolescent Concerns**	_____
Scramble 3:	**Bulimia Consequences**	_____
Scramble 4:	**Components of Moral Behavior**	_____
Scramble 5:	**Kohlberg's Levels of Morality**	_____
	Your Total Points	_____
	Total Possible Points	52
	% =	_____

III.   **Experiencing**

Main Points and Exercises

Exercises
Chapter 11

Adolescence as Transition

1.   In many nonindustrialized (discontinuous) societies, passage from childhood to adulthood is marked by rites of passage, often distinguished by separation, training, initiation (sometimes with scarification and circumcision), and induction into the tribe. Continuous societies have no formal rites of passage (there are some experimental programs in some schools and communities), although some writers claim that secondary schools serve a similar purpose

Exercise 1:   Try to recall a "rite of passage" you went through as an adolescent. List the steps in the separation, training, initiation and induction that were involved. If you do not remember one, ask a friend if they remember. If they cannot remember make up a fantasy one -- perhaps one you have always wanted.

Physical and Biological Changes

2.   There is a spurt in rate of height and weight increase during adolescence, which occurs about two years earlier for girls than for boys. Boys retain relatively less fat mass and, on average, outperform girls on measures of strength, speed, and endurance, although not in rhythmic activities. The changes of *pubescence* (in primary sexual characteristics, directly related to reproduction; and in secondary sexual characteristics, not directly related to reproduction) lead to *puberty* (sexual maturity).

Exercise 2:   You have an 11 year old relative who wants to know what she can expect when she "grows up". Give her your adolescent lecture, telling her about boys and girls during pubescence and puberty.

3.   Early maturation is often advantageous for boys but less so for girls. Pubertal change is most stressful when it puts the adolescent out of step with peers, especially if it is not seen as desirable. Common adolescent concerns include worries about such things as the future, finances, school, appearance, feelings of inferiority, loneliness, the purpose of life, sex, the stability of the parents' marriage, and lack of time.

Exercise 3:   **Imagine** discussing with your own child (a preadolescent) the consequences for early maturation in a male and a female. What would you tell them, not only about the physical changes but the stress that is faced?

Nutrition and Eating Disorders

4.   Because of rapid muscular and skeletal growth, adolescents require large amounts of protein and minerals such as calcium. Most also expend a relatively large number of calories, but obesity is still the most common nutritional problem of adolescents in North America.

Exercise 4:   In your speech class you must give a 3 minute speech on "Obesity". Outline what you would say including definition, causes, control and your personal observation.

5.   Anorexia involves significant weight loss, refusal to maintain weight, and distorted body image. Bulimia is defined in terms of recurrent episodes of binge eating (often followed by "purges") that are accompanied by the realization that the behavior is not normal and by feelings of guilt or self-deprecation. Both anorexia and bulimia are most common among adolescent girls (10 times more girls than boys), are probably associated with our sociocultural emphasis on thinness, and can sometimes be treated with antidepressant drugs or with interventions like cognitive-behavioral therapy.

Exercise 5a: Mildred's mother is afraid her daughter's extreme thinness is due more to attitude than eating. She asks your opinion and you feel it is a chance to explain anorexia nervosa to her. What would you say to her? Define it, give some causes and mostly what could she do about it.

Exercise 5b: Your friend tells you she has a friend who eats a lot and then "throws up". (Splurge and purge) Here is your chance to play expert and describe bulimia. Give the definition, some causes and potential treatment.

Adolescent Intellectual Development

6.   The intellectual development of the adolescent may culminate in thought that is potentially completely logical, is inferential, deals with the hypothetical as well as with the concrete, and is systematic. Formal operations make possible a type of intense idealism that may be reflected in adolescent frustration or rebellion, as well as in more advanced levels of moral orientation.

Exercise 6: Dexter is angry with his 11 year old because he does not use "common sense". You see it is a problem of not understanding the adolescent's intellectual development. Explain to Dexter Piaget's view of formal operations including formal vs. concrete thinking and the implications of formal thinking.

7. Information-processing views of development are concerned with the acquisition of a knowledge base (grows with experience and schooling), the development of information-processing strategies (becomes better and more appropriate with advancing age), and the development of metacognitive skills (increasing understanding of personal processes involved in learning and remembering).

Exercise 7: Senghi is so proud of her 15 year old because she seems to be so "clear headed in her thinking". Here is your chance to explain the three important aspects of cognition: the acquisition of knowledge, the development of information-processing strategies and the development of metacognitive skills. I'm sure Senghi will hope her daughter will grow up to be as brilliant as you.

Adolescent Egocentrism

8. Adolescent egocentrism describes a self-centeredness that leads adolescents to believe that others are highly interested in their thoughts and behaviors (a *self-consciousness*) . It is evident in the *imaginary audience* (an imagined collection of people assumed to be concerned with the adolescent) and the *personal fable* (feelings of invulnerability and uniqueness). Adolescents' greater propensity for taking high risks may be linked to their sense of invulnerability and uniqueness.

Exercise 8: "Some day that kid is gonna kill himself or get into one heck of an accident." If this statement were made to you about an adolescent, how would you respond now that you know about adolescent egocentrism, the imaginary audience and the personal fable? How will you respond when your child gets to be an adolescent?

Moral Development

9.   Carroll and Rest describe four components of moral behavior: (1) recognizing a moral problem (*moral sensitivity*), (2) deciding what ought to be done (*moral judgment*), (3) devising a plan of action according to ideals (*moral values*), and (4) implementing the plan (*moral action*). Failure to act morally may be the result of a deficiency in any one of these four components.

Exercise 9:   Recall a moral decision you were faced with as an adolescent. Go through the 4 components of moral behavior as outlined by Carroll and Rest. Compare it to a moral decision you have recently faced. Are the situations the same? -- different?

10.   Piaget describes morality as progressing from a stage of *heteronomy* (to age 9 or 12; responds to external rewards and punishments) to eventual *autonomy* (after age 10 or so; self-determined principles and ideals) Kohlberg describes progression through three levels, each with two stages: *preconventional* (concerned with self--pain, pleasure, obedience, punishment), *conventional* (concerned with the group, with being liked, with conforming to law), and *postconventional* (concerned with abstract principles, ethics, social contracts). The last level is rare, even among adults; most operate at the conventional level ("I'll be a good boy/girl so you will like me; I'll obey the law because it's the law").

Exercise 10:   You are at a preschool meeting with your mate and the subject or morality in children comes up. You want everyone to know you have thought about the issue. You impress them with your knowledge of Piaget (heteronomy-autonomy) and Kohlberg (preconventional - 2 stages, conventional - 2 stages and conventional - 3 stages). You use the outline you are about to make up. Don't you feel good about having done the outline when you were taking this course?

11.   Gilligan's work suggests that men and women differ in their moral development -- that men become progressively more concerned with law and order whereas women respond more to social relationships and to the social consequences of behavior. Various programs using indoctrination, role playing, and modeling have been successful in increasing levels of moral judgment and, sometimes, moral behavior in students. Parental discipline that points out the harmful consequences of the child's behavior for others, and the frequent expression of parental affection, are also important.

Exercise 11:   Do you agree with Gilligan that there may be a male and female morality? The next time you have the opportunity present it in a situation where both sexes are present and watch the response. Should make you a popular person.

I.   Reading and Understanding

Social Development: Adolescence
Chapter 12

This Chapter
Self and Identity
    --self
    --identity
--The Self in Adolescence
    --self-worth (or self-esteem)
--Self-Image and the Offer Questionnaire
    --self-image
    --self-worth
    --Offer Self Image Questionnaire
    --Offer's Facets of Self
        --Psychological self
        --Social self
        --Sexual self
        --Familial self
        --Coping self
    --The Universal Adolescent
        --Psychological
        --Social
        --Sexual
        --Familial
        --Coping
    --The Context-Bound Adolescent
    --Sturm and Drang?
    --Stress and Life Change
        --negative affect
--The Development of Identity
    --identity versus role diffusion
    --wholeness
    --adolescent moratorium
        --negative identities
    --Identity Diffusion
    --Foreclosure
    --Moratorium Individuals
        --foreclosure
        --identity diffusion
    --Identity Achieved
Social Development in Context
--Parent-Adolescent Relationships
    --distancing
    --emotional distancing
    --buffer
    --Parenting Adolescents
    --Parent-Adolescent Conflict
--Peer Groups
Gender and Gender Roles
    --gender roles
    --gender
    --androgynous
    --gender typing
--Common Gender-Role Stereotypes
    --sexual stereotypes
    --Gender-Role Preference

--Gender Differences
        --Biological Differences
        --Psychological Differences
        --Verbal Ability
        --Visual/Spatial Ability
        --Mathematics and Science
                --from adolescence onward
        --Aggression
                --generally
Sex
--Sexual Beliefs and Behavior
        --The Double Standard
                --sexual double standard
        --Attitudes
        --Age of Initiation
        --Masturbation
--Adolescent Pregnancy
        --Who Gets Pregnant?
        --Why?
        --Implications
        --What to Do?
                --abstinence
        --Homosexuality
--Sexually Transmitted Diseases
        --sexually transmitted diseases (STDs)
                --venereal diseases
        --Chlamydia
        --Gonorrhea
        --Genital herpes
        --AIDS
        --Other STDs
                --pelvic inflammatory disease
Adolescent Turmoil
--Delinquency
        --Delinquent
        --Social Class
        --Intelligence
        --Peers
        --Parents
        --Personality
        --Sex
--adolescent Gangs
        --gang
--Drugs
        --Some Definitions
                --Drug Abuse
                --Drug dependence
                --Physiological dependence
                --Psychological dependence
                --Drug tolerance
                        --Diagnostic and Statistical Manual (DSM-IV)_
        --Who Uses Drugs?
        --Reasons for Drug Use
                --gateway drug-use theory
        --Implications of Teenage Drug Use
                --normal
                --delaying
                --abuse

--Marijuana
      --tetrahydrocannabinol (THC)
--LSD
      --D-lysergic acid diethylamide tartrate (LSD-25)
--Alcohol
--Cocaine
      --speedball
      --illegal
--Other Drugs
--Suicide
    --Rate
    --Sex Differences
    --Psychological Explanations
    --Individual Explanations

II. Learning and Comprehending

Scrambles
Chapter 12

Scramble 1: Match the Five Self Evaluation Questions with the Appropriate Self Aspect

			Points
Psychological Self	1.	_____	_____
	2.	_____	_____
	3.	_____	_____
	4.	_____	_____
	5.	_____	_____
Social Self	1.	_____	_____
	2.	_____	_____
	3.	_____	_____
	4.	_____	_____
	5.	_____	_____
Sexual Self	1.	_____	_____
	2.	_____	_____
	3.	_____	_____
	4.	_____	_____
	5.	_____	_____
Familial Self	1.	_____	_____
	2.	_____	_____
	3.	_____	_____
	4.	_____	_____
	5.	_____	_____
Coping Self	1.	_____	_____
	2.	_____	_____
	3.	_____	_____
	4.	_____	_____

5. _____   _____

Your Total Self   _____
Total Possible Points   25
% =   _____

1.   How do I feel about my parents?
2.   Do I like my body?
3.   Am I well adjusted? Reasonably happy? How decisive am I?
4.   What do I think of pornography?
5.   Am I in control of myself?
6.   Am I friendly?
7.   Do I prefer to stay home?
8.   What school demands?
9.   What are my feelings?
10.   Am I a loner?
11.   How do I feel about my home?
12.   How do I feel about my relatives?
13.   Sexually attractive to them?
14.   How do I feel about my siblings?
15.   How do I feel about sex?
16.   How effective am I?
17.   What are my wishes?
18.   What are my fantasies?
19.   Do people like me?
20.   Comfortable with my sexuality?
21.   What kind of morals do I have?
22.   How well do I cope with what others demand?
23.   What I demand?
24.   Am I outgoing?
25.   Am I sexually attracted to others?

Scramble 2   **Listed below are Marcia's Four Status. List 2 characteristics for each status from the list below.**

Status	Characteristics		Points
Identity diffusion	1.	_____	_____
	2.	_____	_____
Foreclosure	1.	_____	_____
	2.	_____	_____
Moratorium	1.	_____	_____
	2.	_____	_____
Identity Achieved	1.	_____	_____
	2.	_____	_____

Your Total Points   _____
Total Possible Points   8
% =   _____

1.   Crisis
2.   Commitment made
3.   Strong commitment (commitment predetermined by political, social, or religious affiliation)
4.   No crisis
5.   No crisis
6.   No commitment (ambiguous belief systems, no vocational commitment)
7.   No commitment (period of exploration of alternatives)
8.   Crisis finished

Scramble 3: Listed below are the Three Stages of Socialization. Pick the appropriate Stage and Conflict that match each.

Stage	Time Frame	Conflict	Points
_____	**Early Childhood**	_____	_____
_____	**Later Childhood-Early Adolescence**	_____	_____
_____	**Late Childhood-Early Adulthood**	_____	_____

Your Total Points _____
Total Possible Points 6
% = _____

Stage
1. Decreasing dependence on parents and increasing independence
2. High dependence on parents
3. High independence

Conflict
1. Low
2. Decreasing
3. Increasing

Scramble 4: Match the Description with Disease

Disease	Description	Points
Genital herpes	_____	_____
Syphilis	_____	_____
Chlamydia	_____	_____
Gonorrhea	_____	_____
Genital Warts	_____	_____
Acute Pelvic Inflammatory Disease	_____	_____
AIDS	_____	_____

Your Total Points _____
Total Possible Points 7
% = _____

A. 4 million women will die by the year 2000 from this disease
B. Discharge from penis and pain during urination
C. Caused by a virus and is incurable
D. Most common of the SIDs
E. A complication that can result from disease such as gonorrhea and chlamydia
F. Twice as many cases in the United States than there were in 1980
G. Caused by a virus and affect about one million people in the United States each year

Scramble 5:   Listed below are the classes of the most frequently abused drugs. List the examples for each.

Narcotics	Sedatives (downers)	Stimulants	Hallucinogen (etc.)	Inhalants	Points
1._____	1._____	1._____	1._____	1._____	_____
2._____	2._____	2._____	2._____	2._____	_____
3._____	3._____	3._____	3._____	3._____	_____
4._____	4._____	4._____	4._____	4._____	_____
5._____	5._____	5._____	5._____	5._____	_____

Your Total Points   _____
Total Possible Points   20
% =   _____

1.   Marijuana
2.   Barbiturates (Phenobarbital, Seconal, Nembutal)
3.   Heroin
4.   Cocaine
5.   Tranquilizers (Valium, Librium, Vivol)
6.   Paint thinner
7.   Mescaline
8.   Solvents
9.   LSD
10.   PCP
11.   Opium
12.   Alcohol
13.   Morphine
14.   Psilocybin
15.   Glue
16.   Crack
17.   Methadone
18.   Aerosol sprays
19.   Codeine
20.   Amphetamines (Benzedrine, Dexedrine, Methedrine)

Scramble 6: **Listed below are 6 Different Types of Drugs. Place the appropriate Signs and Early Symptoms with the appropriate drug.**

		Points				Points	
Narcotics	1.	_____	**Hallucinogen**	1.	_____	_____	
	2.	_____	**Marijuana**	2.	_____	_____	
	3.	_____	**LSD,PCP**	1.	_____	_____	
		_____	**MDA,STP**	2.	_____	_____	
Sedatives	1.	_____	**Inhalants**	1.	_____	_____	
	2.	_____		2.	_____	_____	
	3.	_____					
		_____					
Stimulants	1.	_____					
	2.	_____	Your Total Points		_____		
	3.	_____	Total Possible Points		20		
	4.	_____	% =		_____		
	5.	_____					
	6.	_____					
	7.	_____					
	8.	_____					

1. Odor on breath and clothing
2. Changes in friends
3. Loss of appetite
4. Excessive activity
5. Traces of white powder around nostrils (heroin is sometimes inhaled)
6. Physical evidence may include cough syrup bottles, syringes, cotton swabs, and spoon or cap for heating heroin
7. Drowsiness
8. Needle marks or scars on arms
9. Symptoms of alcohol consumption with or without odor
10. Chapped, dry lips
11. Mood shifts
12. Animated behavior or its opposite
13. Argumentativeness
14. Poor coordination and speech
15. Odor of glue, solvent, or related substance
16. Physical evidence of plastic gags, rags, glue, or solvent containers
17. Panic
18. Bizarre behavior
19. Scratching or rubbing of nose
20. Irascibility

Scramble Summary

Your Total Points _____
Total Possible Points 86
% = _____

III.   **Experiencing**

Main Points and Exercises

Exercises
Chapter 12

Self and Identity

1.   Global self-worth (or self-esteem)_ reflects how well one likes oneself. Self-evaluations are possible in different areas (for example, the Offer categories of psychological, social familial, coping, and sexual). Adolescence is not generally a period of storm and stress. Rather, the universal adolescent is generally happy and optimistic; caring, concerned, and sociable; confident and open about sexual matters; and strongly positive toward the family. context also leads to some systematic differences among adolescents from different cultures.

Exercise: Consider the categories presented by offer. In retrospect how would you rate your own adolescence in each of these areas. Take a moment to jot down your thoughts.

Psychological Self:

Social Self:

Familial Self

Coping Self:

Sexual Self:

2.   According to Erikson, the major developmental task of adolescence is to develop a sense of identity. Marcia describes four possible identity statuses; *identity diffusion* (early adolescence: no commitment and no identity crisis); *foreclosure* (strong commitment to an imposed identity); *moratorium individuals* (adolescents actively exploring alternative identities; vague, changing commitments); and *identity achieved* (commitment following the crisis of the moratorium).

Exercise 2:   Using Marcia's four possible identity status's think of your adolescent friends and try to remember someone for each status. Where would you place yourself?

Identity diffusion:

Foreclosure:

Moratorium Individuals:

Identity Achieved:

Social Development in Context

3.   Social development progresses from a stage of relative dependence on the parents to a stage of relative independence. The role of parents in adolescence is to provide resources, protect adolescents, guide their development, and serve as advocates for them. Increasing allegiance to peers does not necessarily entail a high degree of parent-adolescent conflict. The

majority of teenagers have good relations with their parents, although one of the developmental tasks of this period involves increasing independence from parents.

Exercise 3: "What do our kids want from us?" asks the parents of two teenagers. Now that this question is answered in Chapter 12 explain to these confused parents the four things teenagers need from their parents and give examples of each. You might consider these same points when raising your own teenagers.

4. The adolescent's acceptance by peers is profoundly important for social and psychological well-being. High-status (well-liked) children tend to be happier, more cheerful, more active, and more successful. Peer groups in schools often sort themselves into "crowds" on the basis of principal interests and behaviors (populars, jocks, brains, normals, druggies, and outcasts).

Exercise 4: Listed below are the 6 groups (crowds) outlined by Brown and colleagues. Try to recall someone from each group. What was your impression of them? Where would you fall?

Populars   Normals

Jocks   Druggies

Brains   Outcasts

Gender and Gender roles

5. Gender refers to characteristics associated with biological sex (masculine or feminine). Stereotypes view the male gender as dominant and active, and the female gender as more passive and nurturant. responses to the "sex-change" question reveal predominantly positive evaluations of the male role and negative evaluations of the female role--by both males and females.

Exercise 5: Research indicates that the male role is seen as positive and the female role seen as negative. For the purposes of this exercises let us consider the positive and negative for both roles. To get a better feeling for the "sex-change" exercise follow the outline below.

For Females	For Males
Five Advantages Being Female	Five Advantages Being Male
1.	1.
2.	2.
3.	3.
4.	4.
5.	5.
Five Disadvantages Being Female	Five Disadvantages Being Male

1.	1.
2.	2.
3.	3.
4.	4.
5.	5.

Five Advantages of Being Male	Five Advantages of Being Female
1.	1.
2.	2.
3.	3.
4.	4.
5.	5.

Five Disadvantages of Being Male	Five Disadvantages of Being Female
1.	1.
2.	2.
3.	3.
4.	4.
5.	5.

Discuss your list with someone in your class from the opposite sex. Are the lists similar-same likes-dislikes?

6. Some gender differences are biological, evident in the greater fragility of the males (higher mortality). Gender differences in mathematics and spatial ability (favoring males) and in verbal ability (favoring females) are small, not usually apparent prior to adolescence, and best explained in terms of culturally determined interests and opportunities rather than in terms of genetically ordained differences.

Exercise 6: Listed below are the 4 areas of psychological differences. Try to recall your adolescent days and place 3 names in each category. do they fit the traditional stereotypic view? Among your present acquaintances would you say the stereotype is true?

Verbal Ability:

Visual/Spatial Ability:

Mathematics and Science:

Aggression:

Sex

7.   The sexual revolution among adolescents is evident in an increase in sexual activity (greater among females than males) and a lowering of the age of first intercourse. Almost half of young adolescents consider sexual relations permissible if partners have been together a number of times and have developed a caring relationship. Approximately 20 percent of sexually active teenage girls become pregnant each year, and almost half give birth. About 40 percent undergo abortions. Teenage parenthood is often associated with disadvantages to both mother (interruption of normal developmental progression) and infant (higher infant mortality, child neglect, developmental problems among children).

Exercise 7:   This exercise consists of several parts. Do them progressively and finish one before moving on to the next.

A.   You have been asked to give a 5-minute talk to a group of teenagers about sex and the sexual revolution. List at least 5 points (do more if you wish) that you would feel important for them to know.

B.   Now that you have completed the list would you change or modify it under any of the circumstances listed below.

   1.   Presenting it in an area known for sexual acting out and a great deal of "sexual freedom"?

   2.   Presenting it to a religious school?

   3.   Presenting it with parents present?

   4.   Presenting it to adolescent girls only?

   5.   Presenting it to adolescent boys only?

C.   Were these points presented to you as a teenager?

D.   Do you feel any of these points would have had an effect upon you if you knew about them?

8.   The Most common sexually transmitted diseases are gonorrhea, herpes, and chlamydia; syphilis and AIDS are rarer. Gonorrhea, chlamydia, and syphilis can be cured with drugs; herpes can sometimes be controlled, but it cannot be cured; AIDS is incurable and fatal.

Exercise 8:   You have an adolescent friend who feels that all this information on sexual diseases is bunk and just a scare tactic by adults. Prepare a convincing rebuttal to the argument mentioning all 7 diseases listed in the book, whether or not they have complications and whether or not it can be cured. How convincing do you feel this argument can be? What facts would have had an influence on you?

Adolescent Turmoil

9.   Delinquency is a legal category defined by juvenile apprehension and conviction of a legal transgression, and associated with social class, sex, self-esteem, intelligence, home, and peer influences (such as gang membership). Gangs, many of which are violent, are cohesive groups defined by confrontation with authority.

Exercise 9:   Your son, Philo, an adolescent, keeps talking about gangs at school. You suspect he is either being pressured or wants to join a gang. Based on what you have learned in the Lifespan Text what would you tell him? How could you present information to turn his desire for a gang into productive behavior?

10.   Incidence of drug use among adolescents appears to have leveled off in recent years, except for use of cocaine. Alcohol is still the drug of choice, nicotine is second, and marijuana is a close third. Drug abuse refers to the recreational use of drugs in which use impairs normal functioning. Drug dependence (physiological or psychological) is manifested in a strong desire to continue taking a drug. Reasons for drug abuse include a complex set of genetic and social-environment factors. Predictors of the likelihood of drug abuse among teenagers include drug use among peers or parents; delinquency; stressful life changes; parental neglect, abuse, or abandonment; and low self-esteem.

Exercise 10:   You have selected for your <u>Speech and Communication</u> class a 5-minute talk on drugs. Combine the information on Tables 12.7 and 12.9 in an outline that will describe not only the drugs but early signs and long term symptoms as well. It is possible that you could be asked to give this speech again and again to interested adolescents.

11. Suicide is uncommon, although its frequency among adolescents has more than doubled in recent decades. More girls than boys attempt suicide, but fewer are successful. Although adolescent suicides are often precipitated by a single event (such as a death of a friend, pregnancy, parental divorce, or arrest), few occur without warning.

Exercise 11: You have an adolescent friend who seems depressed -- a little more severe than the usual. The thought of your friend committing suicide slips through your head. Rather than dismiss it as "impossible" you look for the signs that may indicate it as a possibility. List those signs below. What sign(s) would really trigger your worry and what would you do about it?

12. For most adolescents, life is only occasionally turbulent and stressful; most of the time, it abounds with joy and excitement.

Exercise 12: List 10 things from your own adolescence that are "forever" memories. Share them with an adolescent and see if they already have memories.

I.   Reading and Understanding

Physical and Cognitive Changes: Early Adulthood
Chapter 13

This Chapter
  --Peter Pan syndrome
    --early
    --middle adulthood
    --later adulthood
    --The Lifespan
Early Adulthood
  --youth
  --Early Adulthood
--Developmental Tasks
  --Havighurst's Tasks of Early Adulthood
  --Coleman's Transitional Tasks
    --other-centered
--The Transition
  --youth
Physical Development
--Performance
  --quantitative
  --qualitative
--Flexibility
    --slows
    --prevent
--strength and Stamina
  --regardless of physical activity level
  --stability
--The Senses
  --health
--Exercise and Lifestyle
--Drugs and Stress
  --Some consequences of Stress
  --Individual Responses to Stress
  --Sources of Stress
Sex and Reproduction
--Normal Sexual Responses
--Adult Sexual Behavior in the United States
--Sexual Dysfunctions
  --sexual dysfunction
  --erectile dysfunction
    --vaginismus
    --hyperactive sexual desire
--Infertility
  --amenorrhea
Work and Careers
--Employment: Some Definitions
  --career
  --vocation
  --job
  --occupation
--Occupation
  --vocation
  --work
--Why Work?

II.   Learning and Comprehending

Scrambles
Chapter 13

Scramble 1:   **Scrambled below are Havighurst's Developmental Tasks. Place them in the appropriate period.**

Period		Points
Adolescence	1._____	_____
	2._____	_____
	3._____	_____
	4._____	_____
	5._____	_____
Young Adulthood	1._____	_____
	2._____	_____
	3._____	_____
	4._____	_____
	5._____	_____

	Your Total Points	_____
	Total Possible Points	10
	% =	_____

1. Rearing children
2. Developing conceptual and problem-solving skills
3. Establishing a social network
4. Preparing for marriage and family life
5. Counting and selecting a mate
6. Developing an ethical system to guide behavior
7. Beginning career or occupation
8. Preparing for an economically viable career
9. Accepting the changing physique and using the body effectively
10. Starting a family and assuming parent role

Scramble 2: The skills required for effective transition to adulthood are listed blow. Match what they are useful for.

Self Centered Skills	Useful For	Points
Work and Occupational Skill	_____	_____
Self-management Skills	_____	_____
Consumer Skills	_____	_____
Concentrated Involvement Skills	_____	_____
Other-Centered Skills		
Social Interactions Skills	_____	_____
Skills Related to Management of Others	_____	_____
Cooperative Skills	_____	_____

	Useful For	Points
Your Total Points		_____
Total Possible Points		7
% =		_____

1. Learning how to use and enjoy culture as well as goods
2. Effective commerce in a variety of situations with different people
3. Succeeding in undertakings; making significant contributions in many areas
4. Assuming responsibility for those who are dependent
5. Attaining economic independence
6. Engaging in joint endeavors
7. Making reasonable decisions in the lace of wide choice

Scramble 3: Listed below are 10 Life Events reflecting change. Reassemble them ranking them from 1 to 10 in importance. (Do not refer to your book until you have completed the task.

Life Event:	Rank	Points
1. Sex difficulties	_____	_____
2. Change in sleeping habits	_____	_____
3. Minor violations of the law	_____	_____
4. Marital separation	_____	_____
5. Mortgage over $10,000	_____	_____
6. Revision of personal habits	_____	_____
7. Marriage	_____	_____
8. Outstanding personal achievement	_____	_____
9. Change in recreation	_____	_____
10. Marital reconciliation	_____	_____

	Rank	Points
Your Total Points		_____
Total Possible Points		10
% =		_____

Scramble 4: **Match the Randomized Statements below with the appropriate Dysfunction.**

Dysfunction	Statement	Points
Retarded ejaculation	_____	_____
Vaginismus	_____	_____
Hypoactive sexual desire	_____	_____
Premature ejaculation	_____	_____
Impotence	_____	_____
	Your Total Points	_____
	Total Possible Points	5
	% =	_____

a.   Inability to achieve or maintain an erection
b.   Inability to control ejaculation
c.   Lower than normal interest in sexual activity
d.   Painful intercourse
e.   Inability to achieve orgasm during intercourse

Scramble 5: Listed below is the Job-Person Matching Model based on Holland's Coping Styles. Characteristics and Jobs Settings have been scrambled. Match the Characteristics and Job Settings to the Type.

Type		Characteristics	Recommended Job Settings		Points
Realistic	1.	_____	1.	_____	_____
	2.	_____	1.	_____	_____
Intellectual	1.	_____	1.	_____	_____
	2.	_____	1.	_____	_____
Artistic	1.	_____	1.	_____	_____
	2.	_____	1.	_____	_____
Social	1.	_____	1.	_____	_____
	2.	_____	1.	_____	_____
Enterprising	1.	_____	1.	_____	_____
	2.	_____	1.	_____	_____
Conventional	1.	_____	1.	_____	_____
	2.	_____	1.	_____	_____

Your Total Points _____
Total Possible Points   24
% =   _____

1. Concrete
2. Labor
3. Creative
4. Visual arts
5. Extroverted
6. Leadership roles
7. Banking
8. Research
9. Teaching
10. Farm
11. Abstract
12. Performing arts
13. Business/clerical
14. Want social approval
15. Unimaginative
16. Adventurous
17. Intuitive
18. Mechanically oriented
19. Academics
20. High verbal ability
21. Counseling
22. Subjective
23. Extroverted
24. Real estate development

158

Scramble 6: **Organize and match in the appropriate sequence Ginzberg's Developmental Guidance Models.**

Stage	Approximate Age	Major Career Events	Points
_____	_____	_____	____
_____	_____	_____	____
_____	_____	_____	____

1. Growing awareness of requirements of different careers; increasing realization of personal interests and capabilities; keener awareness of the status and rewards associated with different careers.
2. Fantasy
3. 10-12 to about 16
4. Unrealistic notions of career possibilities; child wants to be a president, an astronaut, a ballerina, an actress, a famous explorer, a cowboy.
5. Late adolescence through early adulthood and even later
6. Realistic
7. To 10 or 12
8. Tentative
9. Involves beginnings of career decisions through active _exploration_ of alternatives; commitment to a clear career choice (_crystallization_); undertaking series of activities necessary for implementing choice (_specification_). for many individuals, the process of career evaluation continues through life, and different career choices may be made in midladder.

Scramble 7: **Listed below are the Subtheories, Components and Detailed Descriptions of Dealing with the Main Aspects of the Intelligence According to Explicit (Triarchic) Theory**

			Points
I		_____	____
	A.		
		1._____	____
		2._____	____
	B.	1._____	____
		2._____	____
II.		_____	____
	A.	1._____	____
		2._____	____
	B.	1._____	____
		2._____	____
III.		_____	____
	A.	1._____	____
		2._____	____
	B.	1._____	____
		2._____	____
	C.	1._____	____
		2._____	____

Your Total Points _____
Total Possible Points 17
% = _____

1. Recognizing existence of a problem
2. Componential Subtheory
3. Performance components (partial list)
4. Experiential subtheory
5. Automatizing information processing
6. Shaping of environment
7. Metacomponents
8. Dealing with relative novelty
9. Selecting lower-order components to solve problem
10. Allocating mental resources
11. Encoding stimuli
12. Selective comparison of new to old information
13. Adaptation to environment
14. Comparing stimuli
15. Contextual Subtheory
16. Selection of environment
17. Knowledge-Acquisition Components

Scramble Summary

		Points
Scramble 1:	Havighurst's Developmental Tasks	_____
Scramble 2:	Transition Skills	_____
Scramble 3:	Life Events Reflecting Change	_____
Scramble 4:	Sexual Dysfunctions	_____
Scramble 5:	Job-Person Matching	_____
Scramble 6:	Ginzberg's Developmental Guidance Model	_____
Scramble 7:	Triarchic Theory	_____

Your Total Points _____
Total Possible Points 82
% = _____

III.   Experiencing

Main Points and Exercises

Exercises
Chapter 13

Early Adulthood

1. The Peter Pan syndrome describes men who have not finished growing up in that they have refused or avoided completing the important developmental tasks (according to Havighurst, sequential milestones that reflect the acquisition of important competencies and responsibilities such as establishing a family and a career) of youth (ages 14 to 24, Coleman).

Exercise 1: Cloe, 24-years-old, is dating a guy 30 who doesn't seem to "grow up." She describes him as a play boy, i.e., he doesn't have a job or want to train for one, not serious about marriage, having kids or even a circle of friends. Sounds to you as if he is manifesting the Peter Pan Syndrome. Explain to Cloe the syndrome and how it is tied to developmental tasks and early adulthood.

2. Transition to adulthood, says Coleman, requires "self-centered" competencies (for example, relating to economic independence), and "other-centered" capabilities (having to do with social interaction and social responsibility).

Exercise 2: Take a moment to look at your own life. What transitions are you going through? What are the ones you have gone through? What ones do you anticipate? Use Tables 13.1 and 13.2 as guidelines.

Physical Development

3. Adulthood is not a plateau according to our current models. Motor performance among males, measured quantitatively (speed of running, distance thrown) usually improves through childhood and adolescence and peaks in early adulthood; among females, there is sometimes a plateau or decline after puberty, associated with limited practice. Qualitative measures show continued improvement of motor performance into adulthood. In the absence of training, flexibility declines gradually from about age 12, but can be maintained and even improved into adulthood with training.

Exercise 3: Ask your parents about quantitative and qualitative changes they have noticed in their physical activity. When did they first notice changes? How did they feel about it? If you have grandparents who are living talk to them about their "younger days" and the changes they have noticed. You may be doing a favor by having them relive the "old" days.

4. There are no dramatic age-related changes in the functioning of the senses through early adulthood, but there are subtle changes in the flexibility of the lens, and gradual, mostly noise-induced hearing loss, especially in men.

162

Exercise 4: The next time you have an opportunity to observe a crowd of people, notice how many of the "older" people wear glasses (thick glasses) and how many have hearing aids. Picture yourself at 45. How would you look with glasses? And a hearing aid? More importantly, how would you feel? How do your parents and grandparents feel about the effects of age on their physical development?

Health

5. In early adulthood, there is a decreased susceptibility to common infections, but a somewhat greater incidence of chronic complaints. Exercise contributes in important ways to physical *and* psychological well-being. Accidents are the principle cause of death prior to age 45, and heart disease and cancer after age 45. Stress is implicated in physical complaints (ulcers, hypertension, cardiovascular problems) as well as in psychological complaints (Type A individuals, who are aggressive and hard-driving, are more likely to suffer from coronary heart disease than Type B's, who are more easygoing and relaxed).

Exercise 5: Listed below is a checklist of Type A and Type B behaviors. Check each behavior that you feel reflects your mother - your father - yourself. Who do you most resemble in this category?

Type A	Mother	Father	Myself
Hard Driving			
Impatient			
Competitive			
Pressure of Time			
Urgency in Life			

Type B	Mother	Father	Myself
Slow			
Relaxed			
Easygoing			
Impose Few Deadlines			
No Sense of Urgency			

Go through the list a second time. Which of your parents (comparing the two) show the characteristics above? Are you like that parent?

Sex and Reproduction

6. The human sexual response cycles through excitement (preparation), plateau (mounting arousal), orgasm, and resolution. Sexual dysfunctions in the male include premature ejaculation, retarded ejaculation, and erectile dysfunction; in the female, hypoactive sex drive, inability to attain orgasm or pleasure from sexual intercourse, and vaginismus. Infertility increases gradually through early adulthood. The most common causes are blocked fallopian tubes in the female (often due to acute pelvic inflammatory disease), and low sperm count in men.

Exercise 6a: Now that you have read the material sex and reproduction in this chapter you can be classified as a "pseudo sex expert," (PSE). As a PSE outline a lecture on the human sexual response cycle that you would be asked to give to a group of young adult couples in a premarriage training class. Clarify how women differ from men in the cycle.

Exercise 6b: As a PSE your job is to lecture to a group of old couples on sexual dysfunctions and infertility. Outline a brief lecture stressing common difficulties of males and females in later adulthood.

Work and Careers

7.   Work serves economic, social, and psychological functions. *Jobs* are specific tasks or duties; *occupation* is a broad employment classification (such as being a mechanic); *career* refers to a range of related occupations; *vocation* refers to a "calling" (like a ministry).

Exercise 7:   On a personal level fill in the following items, even if it is a fantasy. Describe each briefly.

Dream Occupation

Dream Career

Dream Job

Dream Calling

8.   Health-care related jobs are projected to be among the fastest growing; manufacturing and assembling jobs, the fastest declining. A job-person matching approach to career choice (Holland) tries to match individual interests and talents with work requirements; developmental guidance models (Ginzberg, Super) describe sequential stages of exploration and preparation for a career (Ginzberg lists three: *fantasy, tentative, realistic*). In practice, career selection is highly influenced by family and other contextual influences, career self-efficacy expectations (anticipations of being competent and successful), and other factors such as race, sex, economics, and so on. Fortune also plays a role.

Exercise 8a: Your friend Tim, in very young adulthood wants to know where to begin to think about his future work life. Explain to him the theories of Career Choice (job person matching, developmental career models and the lifespan career model).

Exercise 8b: On a persona level, go through the characteristics and interests of Holland's coping styles listed in Table 13.5. Make a list below. Now list the job setting recommended. Do any of the jobs appeal to you? Has this list given you any insight? Has the type of work you have selected fit into the information on this Table?

9.   We ask not only that our jobs fill our bellies but also that they make us happy. Job satisfaction is related to personal interest in the work, the extent to which it requires use of the individual's capabilities, income, and job security.

Exercise 9:   Write a paragraph describing the ideal job for you including your interests, your capabilities, the income and job security.

Cognitive Change

10.   Riegel, Basseches, and Labouvie-Vief suggest that with adulthood there may come an increasing recognition and tolerance of ambiguity, conflict, and contradiction, and the learning of new (dialectical) ways of thinking that allow the ongoing resolution of problems, but that bring into play a variety of important considerations other than simple logic--for example, ethics, feasibility, social implications, and so on.

Exercise 10:   Now that you have read about dialectical thinking (Riegel), dialectical schemata (Basseches) and pragmatic wisdom (Labouvie-Vief) let's try to make it practical by considering an everyday problem. How would the thinking and decision making of an adolescent (using Piaget's schema) differ from a young adult in making a decision in the following area:

A.   Decision to take on a new job.

B.   Decision to become committed to a cause that is unpopular.

C.   Decision to make a household move to a distant city.

11.   Sternberg's triarchic view of intelligence is *componential* (intelligence consists of metacomponents, performance components, and knowledge-acquisition components), *contextual* (intelligence is adaptive in a specific context), and *experiential* (intelligence may be manifested in the application of old learning to new situations). Indications are that contextual and experiential intelligence become more important as individuals age.

Exercise 11:   Your friend Thedwick (an adult) and his son Thornbird (an adolescent) are having a friendly argument as to whether adults or adolescents are smarter. Here is your chance to show YOUR intelligence by explaining Sternberg's theory. Be sure to include componential, contextual, and experiential aspects of intelligence.

A Contextual Reminder

12.   Our observations and conclusions are context specific.

Exercise 12:   Take a moment to compare the intelligence needed to survive in a computer-technology office and a native in the Amazon where the rain forest is being cleared. How would you know who is the brightest? How would thinking involve others--families, relatives, community? How would basic survival differ?

I. Reading and Understanding

Social Development: Early Adulthood
Chapter 14

This Chapter
Psychosocial Development: Erikson
--Intimacy Versus Isolation
      --Relationships with the Opposite Sex
      --Relationships with Parents
--Research on Erikson's Model
      --career consolidation versus self-absorption
      --generative
      --stages
      --changes
      --developmental level or developmental task
Love and Mate Selection
      --love
      --Loving and Liking Scales
--A Model of Love
      --intimacy
      --passion
      --commitment
      --triangular theory of love
--The Rules of Attraction
      --amour
      --propinquity
--Selecting a Mate
Choices of Lifestyle
--Cohabitation
      --Incidence
      --Reasons
      --Who Cohabits?
      --Cohabitation and Later Marriage
--Common-Law Relationships
        --common-law marriage
--Homosexuality
--Singlehood
      --Never-Marrieds
      --The Separated and Divorced
--Communes
Marriage
      --Polygamy
--Premarital Sex
--Extramarital Sex
--Types of Marriage Relationships
      --vitalized
      --financially focused
      --conflicted
      --traditional
      --balanced
      --Marital Discord
      --Marital Satisfaction
      --Who Among the Married Are Happiest?

The Family
--The Life-Cycle Approach: Duvall
        --life cycle
        --family life-cycle
        --Stage 1: To Have Children?
        --Stages 2-5: Child Rearing
                --Stage 2: Infancy
                --Stage 3: Preschool
                --Stage 4: Preteen School Years
                --Stage 5: Teen years
--An Evaluation of the Life-Cycle Approach
Family Violence
--Interspousal Violence
--Sexual Assault and Acquaintance Rape
        --courtship violence
        --date rape
        --acquaintance rape
        --Acquaintance Rape on Campus
                --stranger
                --party
                --date
        --Attitudes Toward Sexual Violence
The Continuing Evolution of Self
        --impulsive self
        --imperial self
        --interpersonal self
        --institutional self
        --interindividual self

II.   Learning and Comprehending

Scrambles
Chapter 14

Scramble 1:   Listed below is Sternberg's Model of Love including the Type of
Relationship the Balance of Components and Possible Attitudes.
Match each appropriately starting at the lowest intensity and going
to the most intense.

Relationship	Balance of Components	Possible Attitudes	Points
_____	_____	_____	_____
_____	_____	_____	_____
_____	_____	_____	_____
_____	_____	_____	_____
_____	_____	_____	_____
_____	_____	_____	_____
_____	_____	_____	_____
_____	_____	_____	_____

Your Total Points   _____
Total Possible Points   24
% =   _____

Relationship		Balance of Components	
1.	Infatuation	1.	Commitment; no passion or intimacy
2.	Empty love	2.	No passion, no intimacy, no commitment
3.	Nonlove	3.	Intimacy; no passion or commitment
4.	Romantic Love	4.	Intimacy and commitment, no passion
5.	Liking	5.	Intimacy, passion, and commitment
6.	Companionate love	6.	Commitment and passion, no intimacy
7.	Fatuous love	7.	Passion and intimacy, no commitment
8.	Consummate love	8.	Passion, no intimacy or commitment

168

Possible Attitude

1. "He's for me; he's the one! At least for the time being."
2. "I need him...can't leave. But I need to talk to you."
3.. "I want him, I like him, I'm his. Forever."
4. "We'll stick it out. But just because of the kids."
5. "She's like a sister! We're in it for the long haul."
6. "Who? I didn't notice him."
7. "She's nice to talk to."
8. "I just want to be with him--physically, you know."

Scramble 2: Match the Marriage Type with the Appropriate Description

Term		Description		Points
1.	Bigamy	1.	Wife permitted more than one husband	_____
2.	Polygyny	2.	One partner	_____
3.	Serial monogamy	3.	More than one partner	_____
4.	Monogamy	4.	Illegally more than one mate	_____
5.	Polygamy	5.	Husband permitted more than one wife	_____
6.	Polyandry	6.	Marry, divorce, remarry	_____
			Your Total Points	_____
			Total Possible Points	6
			% =	_____

Scramble 3: Match the Type of Relationship With the Appropriate Description(s)

Type	Description(s)	Points
Conflicted	_____	_____
Financially Focused	_____	_____
Devitalized	_____	_____
Traditional	_____	_____
Vitalized	_____	_____
Harmonious	_____	_____
Balanced	_____	_____
	Your Total Points	_____
	Total Possible Points	10
	% =	_____

1. Dissatisfied with all aspects of marriage
2. Dissatisfied with all aspects of marriage except financial
3. Satisfied with most aspects of marriage
4. Dissatisfied with communication, personality, conflict resolution
5. High degree of satisfaction with all aspects of marriage
6. High accord with couple related issues
7. High satisfaction with external issue like leisure time activity
8. Dissatisfaction with external issues
9. Stress with interspousal relationship
10. High satisfaction with respect to family and religious values

Scramble 4:   **Place the appropriate Characteristic with the Alternative Nonexclusive Marital Lifestyle.**

Type	Characteristics	Points
Swinging	_____	_____
Extra marital sex	_____	_____
Sexually open marriage	_____	_____
Group marriage	_____	_____
Non sexual extra marital relationship	_____	_____

Your Total Points		_____
Total Possible Points		6
% =		_____

1.   An open arrangement designed to permit sexual adventuring by either or both partners with other individuals in independent relationships that do not threaten the marriage.
2.   An uncommon alternative usually involving four adults (two spouse pairs)
3.   Major concern is with the independence and growth of individual partners and the development of mutually accepted rules governing the relationship
4.   Mostly nonconsensual, secretive, clandestine "sexual affairs" that tend to be of short duration
5.   More open, nonsexual opposite-sex relationships involving dinners and movies, for example, apparently widely approved by college populations.
6.   Concerned with recreational sex rather than with relationships and often involves groups and mate swapping.

Scramble Summary

		Your Points	Total Points
Scramble 1:	**Sternberg's Model of Love**	_____	_____
Scramble 2:	**Marriage Types**	_____	_____
Scramble 3:	**Marital Relationships**	_____	_____
Scramble 4:	**Alternative Marital Lifestyles**	_____	_____

Your Total Points	_____
Total Possible Points	46
% =	_____

III.   Experiencing

Main Points and Exercises

Exercises
Chapter 14

Psychosocial Development: Erikson

1.   According to Erikson's psychosocial theory of stages characterized by basic conflicts and their resolution, the young adult struggles with *intimacy versus isolation* as relationships with parents and peers change. During this period, the young adult strives to achieve intimacy, often through a reciprocated love relationship with someone of the opposite sex.

Exercise 1:   List below the names of three early adult females and three males. Check whether you feel they have achieved intimacy, are isolated or in-between. Write your observations for that conclusion.

Names: Female   Intimate Between Isolated   Behavioral Observations.

1.

2.

3.

Names: Male   Intimate Between Isolated   Behavioral Observations.

1.

2.

3.

Where would you classify yourself in this chart? What are your behavioral observations based upon?

Love and Mate Selection

2.   Liking implies positive evaluation; loving implies absorption, attachment, and intimacy (a capacity for pain as well as ecstasy). Sternberg's model describes eight varieties of love (or nonlove), identifiable on the basis of combinations of *passion* (strong physical desire), *intimacy* (affection, disclosure), and *commitment* (a decision to be in love, to stay together). Important antecedents of interpersonal attraction (which underlies love) include physical attractiveness, similarity, and propinquity (physical proximity).

Exercise 2a: Gilda feels she is truly in love with Hank. She asks you what you think about it. Rather than get mushy about their relationship tell about Sternberg's theory. Go down the checklist of types of relationships, and the balance of components than decide what the scoop is.

Exercise 2b: Rubin has made a loving and liking test and several of the items are on Table 14.1. Make up your own list of items excluding Rubin's. Remember it is loving differentiated from liking.

Choices of Lifestyle

3.   One basic lifestyle choice is to marry or not to marry. Nonmarried lifestyles include singlehood, cohabitation, homosexual relationships, or one of a variety of communes. Singlehood includes the never-married (voluntarily or not), the divorced or separated, and the widowed. More than one in three marriages ends in divorce, but the majority of the divorced remarry. the emotional, social, and economic impact of divorce is sometimes severe (especially the economic impact for women).

Exercise 3:   Listed below are the choices for lifestyles. List a name of someone you know for each of them and make a statement about their adjustment, happiness and productivity as you see it.

Nonmarried:	Name	Observations
A. **Singlehood**		
1. **Never married**	_____	_____
		_____
2. **Divorced**	_____	_____
		_____
3. **Separated**	_____	_____
		_____
B. **Cohabitation**	_____	_____
		_____
C. **Homosexual Relationship**	_____	_____
		_____
D. **Commune**	_____	_____
		_____

Marriage

4.   Marriage is the lifestyle choice of about 95 percent of people. Social standards governing premarital sex have moved from condoning total abstinence, through the period of the double standard (which lingers still), to a period of sexual permissiveness especially where there is affection between partners. Some (though few) marriages tolerate (or even encourage) extramarital sexual encounters.

Exercise 4:   Listed below are the six Alternative Nonexclusive Marital Lifestyles. Put your opinion of each lifestyle, whether you could practice that style and what your response would be if your mate suggested it.

Style	Opinion-Response
Open Marriage	
Extra Marital Sex	
Non Sexual Extramarital Relationships	
Sexually Open Marriage	
Swinging	
Group Marriage	

5.   Enduring marriages may be *vitalized* (high general satisfaction); *devitalized* (high general dissatisfaction); *financially focused* (high dissatisfaction except for financial issues); *conflicted* (continual conflict regarding couple issues; satisfaction with more external issues); *harmonious* (satisfaction regarding couple issues but not external issues); *traditional* (general dissatisfaction except for family and religious issues); or *balanced* (general satisfaction with some problem areas).

Exercise 5a: Listed below are the seven Types of Marriage Relationships. See if you can recall someone for each style of relationship. What would be your response being in such a relationship?

Type	Name of Couple	Response
Vitalized		
Devitalized		
Financially focused		
Conflicted		
Harmonious		
Traditional		
Balanced		

Exercise 5b: In what category would you list your parents? How would they classify themselves? Could you discuss the alternatives with them? do they consider themselves "happily married?"

6.   Factors contributing to marital satisfaction among women include age at first marriage (later is better), education, and socioeconomic status. Among men, occupation, socioeconomic status, and education contribute to marital satisfaction. the more alike (and the more sexually compatible) two people are, the more likely they are to describe their marriage as happy. Frequency of sexual intercourse is highest for several years immediately following marriage.

Exercise 6:   For some reason or another several of your friends have made you into a premarital counselor. They want to know the factors of success in marriage. Here is your chance to shine with your sage remarks about success in marriage including the factor for success in females (age of marriage, education and socioeconomic status) and males (occupation, socioeconomic status, and education. And, of course, you want to mention (delicately) sexual satisfaction)

The Family

7.   The family can be described in terms of a life cycle with eight task-defined stages: the initial childless years (important tasks center on whether or not to have children, and other career and self-related developmental tasks); the first child; the phase of the preschool child; a school-aged phase (seven years); a teenager phase (seven years); a "launching" phase (eight years); the empty nest to retirement period (15 years), and a retirement-until-death phase. Although this life-cycle approach is useful, it does not apply to nontraditional, increasingly common family groupings (like single-parent families). Nor is it sensitive to differences related to family occupations, social status attitudes, family size, and so on.

Exercise 7:   Here is a chance to become better acquainted with the trials and tribulations faced by your folks in raising a family. The first five stages are listed below. Talk to your mother and father about each stage and what they had to go through. It might be a good idea about fantasizing about what you may go through.

<u>**Your Folks Comments**</u>

Stage 1:   **To have children**

Stage 2:   **Infancy**

Stage 3:   **Preschool**

Stage 4:   Teen Years

Family Violence

8.   Incidence of many types of violent crimes continues to increase, almost half of them perpetrated by acquaintances or relatives of the victim. It is evident in interspousal violence, child abuse, and sexual assault, including date rape. Prevailing social attitudes about the permissibility of physical punishment and stereotypes of male dominance contribute to violence in the family.

Exercise 8:   Assume you have been asked to give a brief talk on "rape on campus" to a senior high school coed group. Combining Ward and associates four types of rape and the type of experience from Table 14.5 what would you include? What do you feel would be critical for high school students to know.

The Continuing Evolution of Self

9.   Kegan's five selves, in order of their evolution, are *impulsive* (concerned with gratification of impulses), *imperial* (oriented toward developing personal competence and achieving control), *interpersonal* (concerned with reciprocal relationships), *institutional* (embedded in work, love, and culture), and *interindividual* (oriented toward adult relationships).

Exercise 9:   Here is an opportunity to make a check on self evolution. Listed below are Kegan's five selves. Write a brief paragraph on each, describing where you were, where you are and where (and how) you want to be.

Impulsive Self

Imperial Self

Interpersonal Self

Institutional Self

Interindividual Self

Physical and Cognitive Development: Middle Adulthood
Chapter 15

This Chapter
Middle Adulthood
--Some Tasks of Middle Adulthood
Physical Changes
--Appearance
--The Senses
        --glaucoma
        --cataracts
        --presbycusis
--Health and Organ Function
        --atherosclerosis
        --arteriosclerosis
            --stroke
        --osteoporosis
--Diet and Exercise
--The Climacteric and Menopause
        --change of life
        --A Physiological Event
            --menopause
        --Nonphysiological Symptoms
            --climacteric syndrome
        --Treatment
            - --estrogen replacement therapy (ERT)
--Sexuality
Cognitive Changes
--Does IQ Change with Age?
--The Evidence
        --Cross-Sectional Studies
        --cohort
        --Longitudinal Studies
        --Sequential Studies
            --sequential designs
--A Conclusion
        --fluid intelligence
        --crystallized intelligence
        --Decline and Stability
--Thinking in Middle Adulthood
        --intuition
        --pragmatics
        --dialectical thinkers
        --dialectical schemata
--Creativity in the Middle Years
        qualitative
Work
--Women in the Workplace
--Male-Female Differences at Work
--Social Changes
--Dual Careers
        --dual-career family
        --Double Careers
            --double-track career
            --burnout

--Career Changes
      --Voluntary Career Changes
         --career self-efficacy
      --Involuntary Career Changes
Leisure

II.   **Learning and Comprehending**

Scrambles
Chapter 15

Scramble 1:   You remember Havighurst. He was back in Chapter 2. Well, his challenges for middle adulthood are still the same so as a reminder list 5 of his 7 challenges that you remember without referring to the chart.

<u>Challenges</u>   <u>Points</u>

1.   _____   _____

2.   _____   _____

3.   _____   _____

4.   _____   _____

5.   _____   _____

                                                        Your Total Points   _____
                                                        Total Possible Points   5
                                                        % =   _____

Scramble Summary

	Your Points	Total Possible Points
Scramble 1: **Havighurst's Challenges**	_____	5

                                    Your Total Points   _____
                                    Total Possible Points 5
                                    % =   _____

178

III.   **Experiencing**

Main Points and Exercises

Exercises
Chapter 15

Middle Adulthood

1.   Middle adulthood is a two-decade period from around 40 or 45 to 60 or 65. Relevant developmental tasks include emptying the nest, maintaining a career, adjusting to the physiological changes of middle age, and maintaining changing relationships with children, spouse, and parents.

Exercise 1:   Think of someone you know going through middle adulthood (perhaps your parents). How many of the challenges to middle adulthood (advocated by Havighurst) do you witness? Can you imagine going through this period? How would it be different from what they are doing?

Physical Changes

2.   Physical changes of middle age include cessation of growth in height (a slight decrement in later years) the accumulation of fatty tissue, loss of skin elasticity, thinning of hair stiffening of joints, loss of muscle tone, and reduction in muscle tissue. Sensory changes include a gradual reduction in visual acuity, greater farsightedness, and a gradual loss of hearing ability, particularly for higher tones.

Exercise 2a: Get a picture of your parents when they were younger (adolescence or young adulthood). Assuming they are now in middle adulthood what specific changes do you see in your mother? List them below. What specific changes to you see in your father? List them below.

Mother Changes   Father Changes

Exercise 2b: Now consider yourself to be in middle adulthood. (Take an old photo and put some wrinkles, lines, fat folds, etc., on your body) and imagine what you will look like at 60-65. Now you can take time to deny you will ever look that way. (P.S. keep the photo until you get to be 60-65, then talk).

3.   Major organ systems slowly become less efficient after early adulthood. Signs of arteriosclerosis (hardening of artery walls) are common, and people become more susceptible to heart disease, cancer, arthritis, cirrhosis, hypertension, and osteoporosis, but less susceptible to acute infections. Diet and exercise can contribute significantly to reducing and delaying some of the effects of aging.

Exercise 3: How many people do you know in middle adulthood? Try to put into two categories those who exercise and are diet conscious and those who are not. Do you notice a difference - not only in their appearance but attitude as well? Are members of your family exercise or diet conscious and do you think it makes a difference?

4. By the late thirties or early forties for women, and perhaps by the fifties for men, the sex glands' production of hormones decreases, leading to the *climacteric* or "change of life" (not dramatic among men; cessation of menstruation, or *menopause,* among women). Menopause is sometimes accompanied by physical symptoms ("hot flashes," trembling, dizziness, and headaches) that are occasionally treated with hormone replacements. Sexual interest and functioning are ordinarily maintained after the climacteric (some reduction in vaginal lubrication for women; slower sexual arousal for men).

Exercise 4: Assuming your role as PSC (Pseudo Sex Counselor) what kind of information would you give a middle couple on what they might anticipate sexually in their later years? List five points that you feel would be important information for them to know.

1.

2.

3.

4.

5.

Cognitive Changes

5. Cross-sectional studies find cohort-related evidence of intellectual decline with age. Longitudinal studies show that abilities dependent on experience (*crystallized)* verbal and numerical abilities, for example) tend not to decline. In contrast, abilities less dependent on experience (*fluid,* like reasoning or attention span) do not fare as well. Significant gains in measured IQ have been observed well into middle age.

Exercise 5: Knowing what you know now about fluid and crystallized intelligence what would you tell Bernice an advanced middle aged adult who keeps saying, "I'm just not as intellectually sharp as I use to be".

6. Middle-aged thinking profits from the greater experience of adults, their increased sensitivity to contradictions, and their responsiveness to social, political, and economic realities. Peak years for creative output in fields where production depends on information and experience are the middle-age years. In areas that require physical strength and stamina (athletics) or culturally defined physical attractiveness (modeling), peak performance occurs at young ages.

Exercise 6:   Take a moment to review some conversations you have had with some middle aged adults. What do you remember about their view points that were different from yours? Do you notice a difference in middle adulthood thinking from yours (assuming you are not in middle adulthood)? Take a moment to make a list of differences especially those you feel are unique.

Work

7.   The percentage of adult women who work has more than doubled in this century. More than half of two-parent families have two wage earners. Some involve *dual careers* (husband and wife have independent, equal careers); many involve *double careers* (inequitable division of home-making, child-rearing responsibilities so that one partner, usually the wife, juggles two careers). Women's occupations still tend to be lower than men's in status and income, and still reflect many old stereotypes.

Exercise 7a: List the number of female relatives you have that are either in early or middle adulthood. How many are presently working in or toward a career? How many are involved in a dual or double career? How are the household chores handled?

Exercise 7b: If you are a male how would you feel about your wife working? If you are a female how do you feel having a career and marriage? What do you see as problems to be overcome? For both male and females - how will both parties working influence your choice of mate?

8.   Children in homes where both parents work are not at a measurable disadvantage. voluntary career changes throughout the lifespan may occur in response to the occasional crises of the middle years or because of changes in the work context (such as technological changes) or the individual (for example, emptying of the family nest). Involuntary changes can be related to being fired, external changes in the workplace, advancing age for "early-leaver" careers, illness or injury, or mandatory retirement.

Exercise 8:   List the names of three people you know who have had a voluntary career change. Now list three people who have made an involuntary career change. What were their reactions to the change? Do you notice a generalized reaction difference between the two groups?

1.

2.

3.

Leisure

9.   Leisure, discretionary time, is important for psychological health and happiness and, like work, can contribute significantly to our identities and to our feelings of worth. Besides, if we smell no roses before we retire, the ones we could have smelled will be gone, and we may not have learned where the new ones grow.

Exercise 9:   It's time for another personal inventory check. How much time do you put aside for leisure? What type of leisure are you most interested in? How do you feel about "doing nothing," or having free time? Do you plan to put aside leisure time? If you were given leisure time on the job - what would you do?

I. Reading and Understanding

Social Development: Middle Adulthood
Chapter 16

This Chapter
Descriptions of Middle Adulthood
--Generativity Versus Self-Absorption: Erikson
     --intimacy versus isolation
     --middle adult years
     --generativity versus self-absorption
--Elaborating Erikson: Peck
     --Valuing Wisdom Versus Valuing Physical Powers
     --Socializing Versus Sexuality
     --Emotional Flexibility Versus Emotional Impoverishment
     --Mental Flexibility Versus Mental Rigidity
Seasons of a Man's Life: Levinson
     --Early Adulthood
     --Levinson's dream
          --age 30 transition
          --settling down
     --The Midlife Transition
          --midlife crisis
          --purpose in life
     --Entering Middle Adulthood
     --Age 50 Transition
     --Culmination of Middle Adulthood
--Seasons of a Woman's Life: Levinson
     --Gender-Based Dreams
          --gender-splitting
     --Career Transition
--Sheehy's Passages
     --crisis
     --passages
     --deadline decade
     --Male-Female Differences at Midlife
-     --freestyle fifties
     --thoughtful seventies
     --proud-to-be eighties
--Gould's Transformations
     --self-consciousness
--Is There a Midlife Crisis?
     --midlife crisis
     --midlife identity crisis
     --universal crisis
Family Relationships
--Relationships with Children
     --Launching
          --launching phase
     --The Empty Nest
          --empty nest phase
--Relationships with Aging Parents

II. Learning and Comprehending

Scrambles
Chapter 16

Scramble 1: Match the conflicts for middle age as outlined by Peck.

			Points
_____	**Versus**	_____	____
_____	**Versus**	_____	____
_____	**Versus**	_____	____
_____	**Versus**	_____	____

Your Total Points	_____
Total Possible Points	4
% =	_____

1. Mental Rigidity
2. Sexuality
3. Valuing Wisdom
4. Emotional Flexibility

5. Socializing
6. Emotional Impoverishment
7. Valuing Physical Powers
8. Mental Flexibility

Scramble 2: Listed below are Sheehy's Adult Transactions. Match the Passage Label and Ages with the appropriate Principal Task and Characteristics

Passage Label	Principal Tasks and Characteristics	Points
Pulling Up Roots (18-22)	_____	____
The Trying Twenties (23-27)	_____	____
Catch 30 (28-33)	_____	____
Deadline Decade (35-45)	_____	____
The Comeback Decade (46-55)	_____	____
The Freestyle Fifties (50s)	_____	____
The Selective Sixties (60s)	_____	____
The Thoughtful Seventies (70s)	_____	____
The Proud-to-Be Eighties (80s)	_____	____

Your Total Points	_____
Total Possible Points	9
% =	_____

1. Midlife crisis; realization of mortality; reexamination of youthful illusions and dream; turmoil
2. Separating individual from that of parents; leaving security of parental home
3. Phenomenon of second life; movement from stagnation to peak excitement; for men, more interest and enjoyment in environment and social relationships; for woman, more aggressive, managerial commitments
4. Ability to separate the truly important from the trivial; development of distinctive personality; possibility of high excitement about life
5. Detached contemplation; need to find balance between demanding and giving help and comfort; pride in survival and in continued competence
6. Healthiest and happiest individuals are independent, highly involved, and plan ahead. Highly developed ability to think abstractly

7. Danger zone; need to balance work and play, time lived with time left, and changes in placement within generations
8. Emphasis on stability and on "making it", rooting and extending; first sense of stagnation

Scramble 3: **Listed below is Gould's Transformation. Match the with the Major False Assumption and Major Tasks.**

Age	Major False Assumption	Major Tasks	Points
16-22	_____	_____	_____
22-28	_____	_____	_____
28-34	_____	_____	_____
34-45	_____	_____	_____

Your Total Points _____
Total Possible Points 8
% = _____

Major False Assumptions
1. "If I want to succeed, I need to succeed, I need to do things the way my parents do." "If I make mistakes and need rescuing, they'll rescue me."
2. "Life is pretty straightforward, especially if you're on the right track. There aren't too many contradictions."
3. "I have all the time I need. I am doing the right thing."
4. "My parents will always be my parents. I'll always believe in them."

Major Tasks
1. Recognize and accept idea of one's own mortality; develop strong sense of personal responsibility; reassess values and priorities
2. Become independent; explore adult roles; abandon idea that things will always turn out right if done in the manner of parents.
3. Explore aspects of inner self; become more sensitive to emotions; begin to realize inner contradictions
4. Move away from home; abandon idea that parents are always right

Scramble Summary

		Your Points	Total Possible Points
Scramble 1:	**Peck's Middle Age Conflicts**	_____	4
Scramble 2:	**Sheehy's Adult Transitions**	_____	9
Scramble 3:	**Gould's Transformations**	_____	8
	Your Total Points	_____	
	Total Possible Points	21	
	% =	_____	

III.   **Experiencing**

Main Points and Exercises

Exercises
Chapter 16

Descriptions of Middle Adulthood

1.   Erikson describes the conflict of the middle years as one of *generativity* (being productive in work, community, family) *versus self-absorption* (temptation to become self-absorbed). Peck elaborates Erikson's last two major stages, adding for middle adulthood *valuing wisdom versus valuing physical powers, socializing versus sexuality, emotional flexibility versus emotional impoverishment,* and *mental flexibility versus mental rigidity.*

Exercise 1a: Think of five middle adulthood individuals you know. Using Erikson's generativity vs. self absorption concept, who many would you say have resolved that conflict? How many have not. List the names below and give a brief description of behavior to support your contention.

Individuals   Observations

1.

2.

3.

4.

5.

Exercise 1b: Using the same model as above apply Peck's revision of Erikson's theory to the same individuals. Do it for each of the four conflicts.

Individuals   Observations

1.

2.

3.

4.

5.

2.   Levinson describes several developmental phases, each with important tasks (such as leaving home and making lifestyle decisions) in the early and middle adulthood *seasons* of our lives. Between these phases are important transition periods (ages 20, 30, 40, 50, and so on), the most highly popularized of which is the *midlife transition,* which entails a serious reexamination of the individual's life, particularly in relation to the "dream." Women's dreams are different from men's (concerned with both career and family), reflecting *gender-splitting.*

Exercise 2a: Discuss with each of your parents their "dream" as described by Levinson. Were you aware of their dream?

Exercise 2b: What is your dream? How do you manifest it? Where do you think it will lead you? What would you be like if your dream came true?

3.   Sheehy's lifespan *passages* give the midlife crisis a wider age range (30 to 50), place it earlier for women than for men, and recognize that resolution of the midlife crisis often results in a "turning inward" among men and the opposite among women. Happiness, she argues, is associated with age (older is better), love (married people are happier), and enjoyment of work.

Exercise 3:   You have decided to review Gail Sheehy's book "Passages" for your iteration class. Assuming you had to give a five minute book report - what would you include? How would you summarize the material on Table 16.1 in an oral book report?

4.   Gould describes several *transformations* whereby a childish consciousness, characterized by false and immature assumptions (particularly concerning parents), is gradually replaced by a more adult consciousness.

Exercise 4:   Your friend Fabian, a middle adulthood friend is talking about how foolish he was when he was young. Let's see how subtle you can be in telling him about Gould's transformation. Tie the major false assumption to a major task, remember you will have to live through it yourself some day.

5.   Research suggests that midlife crises are tied more to events than to age and that the majority of individuals do *not* have a full-blown crisis during middle age. But some do.

Exercise 5:   Do you believe in a midlife crisis? Ask your parents and/or other middle adulthood people you know if they have gone through one. See if the females have gone through a more difficult one than males as described in the book.

Family Relationships

6.   Middle age in Duvall's family life cycle includes the *launching phase* (from first to last child leaving home) and the *empty nest phase* (from last child leaving to retirement). Relationships with departed children tend to remain close, and the empty nest does not ordinarily lead to serious unhappiness. Relationships of middle-aged individuals with their aging parents also tend to be warm, and often require caring for them, and adjusting to their dying.

Exercise 6:   Has there been a launching and empty nest phase in your home? If there has been what has been the reaction of your parents? If it hasn't happened has your family discussed it? Do your mother and father differ in their reactions? What do you think will be the reaction when there is truly an empty nest? Do your mother and father discuss it?

7.   Divorce in middle age is less common than at earlier ages and is often harder for women. Remarriage is more common for men than for women after a middle-age divorce (diminishing pool of men). Remarriages in the middle years bring substantial emotional, and sometimes economic, benefits, but may require major readjustments, especially if children are involved. Neither stepparents nor stepchildren easily accept stepkin emotionally as an integral part of their family.

Exercise 7a: Do you know someone recently divorced? Have you discussed it with them? If it is a female does she seem more affected by it than her male counterpart? If it is a male does he seem less affected? If your parents are divorced have you discussed it with them? If they have remarried what are the responses? What is your reaction to the divorce? If your parents are not divorced do you have a friend who has parents who have been divorced? What is their reaction? Does their family discuss it?

Exercise 7b: If your parents are divorced and remarried (one or both parents) what is your reaction to your parents as well as step parents? Are you able to discuss divorce? If your parents are not divorced do you have a friend in this situation? How do they view the divorce situation?

Stability and Change in Middle Age

8.   Some research suggests that males and females become less gender typed and more androgynous through middle age. The magnitude of these changes is very small. Longitudinal investigations of personality change using sequential designs support the hypothesis that there is far more stability than change with age.

Exercise 8:   Two of your middle aged friends, Biff and Bobo, know you are taking the Lifespan Development course and one day they put you on the spot by asking you -- "What can we expect of each other as we go through middle age?" Without batting an eyelash you tell them about androgyny and how Biff will become more feminine and Bobo more masculine. How would you phrase it to be acceptable?

Happiness and Satisfaction

9.   Satisfaction relates to the extent to which various objective aspects of our lives correspond with our goals and aspirations. Happiness is an emotional state, susceptible to fluctuations of mood. Married individuals report more happiness than those who are alone (single, widowed, or divorced); childless couples report as much happiness as those with children; couples whose children have left home (the empty nest) do not, as a result, report lower levels of happiness; and perceived health is closely related to happiness. But psychology does not yet have a complete recipe for happiness.

Exercise 9a: Let us assume that by some magical means you have been given the opportunity to select five things that would make you happy. (We might guess, of course that being rich would be your first one and so exclude it.) Select those items on a personal level that would bring about this emotion. Give a reason for each.

Happiness Selection   Reason

A.
B.
C.
D.
E.

Exercise 9b: What would make your parents happy? How does it differ from your list?

Exercise 9c: List three people you know (or feel) are happy. What leads you to that conclusion?

Happy Person   Reason

A.
B.
C.

Exercise 9d: What do you do now that makes you truly happy? Do you make time for it or does it just occur?

I.   Reading and Understanding

Physical and Cognitive Development: Late Adulthood
Chapter 17

This Chapter
Ageism
--Examples of Ageism
--Social Treatment and Media Portrayal
--Child-Directed Speech
--Ageism and Other Negative Attitudes
Late Adulthood: Who and How Many?
--Dividing Up Old Age
--Changing Demographics
Lifespan and Life Expectancy
--Theories of Biological Aging
        --lifespans
        --life expectancy
        --Genetic Theory
            --genetic theory of aging
        --Cell Malfunction Theories
            --cell error theory
            --toxin theory of cell malfunction
            --radical theory
            --linking theory
        --Organ and System Theories
            --autoimmunity
--Longevity in North America
--Longevity Elsewhere
Physical Changes
        --Senescence
        --Primary aging
        --Appearance
        --Fitness and Exercise
        --Health
            --Parkinson's disease
            --Acute brain syndrome
        --Alzheimer's Disease
--Sensory Changes
        --Vision
        --Hearing
        --Other Senses
--Reaction Time and Attention Span
--Sexuality
Cognitive Changes
--Memory
        --Divisions of Memory
            --short-term memory
            --long-term memory
            --declarative memory
            --semantic memory
            --episodic memory
            --nondeclarative memory
        --Short Term Memory
            --digit-span test
        --Nondeclarative Memory

Episodic and Semantic Memory
--Intelligence
        --Decline or Stability
        --IQ Fluctuations and Terminal Drop
                --terminal drop
--Problem Finding and Intuition
        --Mythical Thinking: Mythos
                --mythos
        --Competence of the Elderly
--Learning in Adulthood
Wisdom
--Some Philosophical Conceptions
--Psychological Conceptions
        --Wisdom and Age
                --intuitive
                --pragmatic
                --understanding
                --gentle
                --sense of humor
                --experienced
                --knowledgeable
                --dialectic
The Implications of Physical and Cognitive Change

II. Learning and Comprehending

Scrambles
Chapter 17

Scrambles 1: **Scrambled below are reasons we die. Match the Theory with the Explanation.**

Theory	Explanation	Points
Cross-linking	_____	_____
Immune system breakdown	_____	_____
Genetic	_____	_____
Toxin	_____	_____
Cell error	_____	_____
Free-radical	_____	_____

Your Total Points	_____	
Total Possible Points	6	
% =	_____	

Explanation

1. The gradual buildup of foreign material in the cells eventually becomes toxic and the cell dies
2. Bonds form among cells, changing their properties and altering their functioning
3. Immune system weakens with age and provides less protection against viral and bacterial invasion or, in a process known as autoimmunity, loses the ability to recognize foreign invaders and begins to attack the system it previously protected
4. Cells are preprogrammed to die
5. Portions of cells become detached, interact with various chemicals and enzymes, and eventually impede the cells' ability to function normally
6. Cellular changes lead to cells becoming nonfunctional as a result of errors that occur in DNA material over time

Scramble 2: **Your book lists 18 ways to live longer. Without referring back to Table 17.3 see if you can remember.**

	Points			Points
1.	_____		8.	_____
2.	_____		9.	_____
3.	_____		10.	_____
4.	_____		11.	_____
5.	_____		12.	_____
6.	_____		13.	_____
7.	_____		14.	_____

Your Total Points	_____	
Total Possible Points	14	
% =	_____	

Scramble 3:   Match the Type of Memory with the Appropriate Description.

Type of Memory		Description		Points
Semantic	_____	1.	Attention span	_____
Nondeclarative	_____	2.	Conscious or explicit	_____
Long term	_____	3.	Autobiographical	_____
Episodic	_____	4.	Non verbalized or implicit	_____
Short term	_____	5.	Stable, abstract	_____
Declarative	_____	6.	All our knowledge base	_____

Your Total Points _____
Total Possible Points   6
% =   _____

Scramble Summary

		Your Total Points	Total Possible Points
Scramble 1:	**Theories of Why We Die**	_____	6
Scramble 2:	**Ways to Live Longer**	_____	14
Scramble 3:	**Memory Types**	_____	6

Your Total Points _____
Total Possible Points   26
% =   _____

III. Experiencing

Main Points and Exercises

Exercises
Chapter 17

Ageism

1. The elderly are often the object of *ageism* (negative prejudices that are based solely on age), evident in media portrayals, in expected behaviors, and in child-directed speech.

Exercise 1: List five movies or TV shows you remember in which ageism was evident. How was it negatively depicted?

1.

2.

3

4.
5.

Late Adulthood: Who and How Many?

2. Old age is socially defined as beginning at age 65. The proportion of people over 65 in the United States has increased fivefold in this century, while the entire population has slightly more than doubled.

Exercise 2: How many people do you know over 65 years of age? List as many as you can below along with the characteristics you admire most in them.

a.,

b.

c.

d.

e.

Lifespan and Life Expectancy

3. Life expectancies (but not lifespans) have increased nearly 50 percent since the turn of this century. In the industrialized world, women can expect to live about eight years longer than men. Aging may be due to a combination of genetic factors (lifespan limits are programmed in cells), cell malfunctions (cell errors, toxins, free radicals, or cross-linked cells hamper normal cell functioning), or immune system defects. Longevity is related to sex, race, mobility, education occupation, employment, locale, heredity, and other factors such as cultural expectations, attitudes toward aging, and lifestyle.

Exercise 3a: Your old Aunt Nellie just doesn't know why she is able to live so long while a lot of her friends have passed away. Here is your chance to show what you have learned about biological aging in the Lifespan Development class. Explain the six theories to her and why she is so lucky.

Exercise 3b: Of the 18 things listed on table 17.3, how many are in your favor to live longer? How many not in your favor? How many do you have control over? How many are out of your control? How many could you change in order to lengthen your life?

4. *Senescence* describes biological decline as a function of age. Among nearly universal characteristics of aging are arteriosclerosis and increased susceptibility to cancer, arthritis and acute brain syndrome. Visible physical changes of age include loss of skin elasticity and consequent wrinkling, loss of hair or hair pigmentation, and loss of teeth or recession of gums, and loss of strength, stamina, and flexibility, much of which can be prevented or moderated through exercise. The elderly are less susceptible to acute infections but more prone to chronic conditions (arthritis, hearing losses, heart disease, visual impairment, and arteriosclerosis), as well as to diseases like Alzheimer's (brain deterioration characterized by memory loss, disorientation, and eventual death).

Exercise 4: What has been the pattern of senescence in your family? Ask your parents about your grandparents and determine which of the conditions have affected them. As a further check, do your parents remember their grandparents and were there the same family conditions? If there is a trend--do your parents expect the same condition? What are the similarities on your mothers and father's side? What are the differences on your mother and father's side?

5. The elderly become more farsighted, may suffer hearing loss and reduced taste and smell sensitivity, and may not react as quickly mentally or physically. Age-related changes in sexual functioning among women include diminished lubrication and loss of vaginal elasticity; in males, changes include greater time for achieving an erection and orgasm, and decline in the force of ejaculation and the intensity of orgasm. Old age brings some decline in sexual interest and activity, but in most cases, sexual activity can continue well into old age.

Exercise 5: You hear your friend Dick say, "My grandparents don't know anything about sex. That's long gone for them." Here is your chance to set him straight about sexuality in the late adulthood stage and to change his perspective - cognitive changes. Use the information on Table 17.7 as evidence.

Cognitive Changes

6. Short-term memory is not dramatically altered by the passage of time, although its capacity may slowly diminish. Procedural (how to do things) and semantic (abstract knowledge) memory are quite resilient; episodic (autobiographical) memory suffers. Declines are most apparent under timed conditions with nonmeaningful material.

Exercise 6: Try to remember your last conversation with an individual in late adulthood (your grandparents perhaps). Did you notice a difference in their short term memory? Procedural, episodic or semantic memory? The next time you are with them you may wish to notice the changes.

7. Age differences in intellectual performance in cross-sectional studies reflect cohort differences (for example, those related to education). Longitudinal studies find little general decline before age 67, with most of the decline in fluid abilities (attention span, speeded abstract tasks); crystallized abilities (dependent on experience) sometimes continue to increase in old age Declines on measures of intelligence might reflect problems of performance rather than lack of competence. Just prior to dying, measured IQ sometimes drops (*terminal drop)*, perhaps because of health problems or *disengagement.*

Exercise 7: Continuing with the question posed in exercise 6 did you notice a difference in fluid versus crystallized intelligence? Was it possible to discuss current events? Recently past events? General facts? Where were you impressed with their knowledge and where were you concerned? Did you find it difficulty to carry on a conversation and did they seem uncomfortable?

8. Older adults often do not do as well as younger individuals on tasks requiring abstract reasoning. Labouvie-Vief describes the thinking of older adults as more intuitive and more personal (*mythos)* rather than formal and logical (*logos)*. Adult learning is a fast-growing field of education that reflects well the capabilities, interests, and enthusiasm of many older people.

Exercise 8a: Again, carrying on from questions 6 and 7 did you find the conversation dealing with things more intuitive and personal (mythos) rather than formal and logical?

Exercise 8b: As a personal exercise try to practice a conversation as would an adult in the late stages thinking mostly of intuitive personal things rather than formality on logic.

Wisdom

9. Wisdom is one of the positive qualities we typically associate with old age. The characteristics of dialectical thinking (openness to contradiction, recognition of the relative nature of knowledge, emphasis on context and pragmatics, acceptance of uncertainty) are closely related to what psychologists think of as wise decision making.

Exercise 9: If you can, list five people you know (or feel) have wisdom. For each of them answer the following questions.

a. Pick one observation on which you base your judgment.

b. Would you go to them and ask advise on an important personal issue?

c. Do others view them as having wisdom?

d. Do you know if others listen and follow what they say?

The Implications of Physical and Cognitive Change

10.   Elderly adults, on average, adjust well to aging. The majority continue to experience joy and happiness in their lives.

Exercise 10:   List five late adults you know and answer the following questions for each.

a.   Do you believe they are happy?

b.   List a traumatic event they have had in their life and the way they have responded to it.

c.   What single thing brings joy to their life?

I.   Reading and Understanding

Social Development: Late Adulthood
Chapter 18

This Chapter
Views of Development in Late Adulthood
--Integrity Versus Despair: Erikson
--Peck's Elaboration of Erikson
       --Ego Differentiation Versus Work-Role Preoccupation
       --Body Transcendence Versus Body Preoccupation
       --Ego Transcendence Versus Ego Preoccupation
--Fisher's Five Periods of Older Adulthood
       --1.   Continuity with Middle Age
       --2.   Early Transition
       --3.   Revised Lifestyle
       --4.   Later Transition
       --5.   Final Period
The Life Review
--Personal Narratives
       --Personal Narratives of the Elderly
           --Reminiscence
       --Life Review Through the Lifespan
--Satisfaction and the Life Review
Retirement
--The Future
--Attitudes Toward and Effects of Retirement
--Phases of Retirement
       --Preretirement
       --Honeymoon
       --Rest and Relaxation
       --Disenchantment
       --Reorientation
       --Routine
       --Termination
Successful Aging
--Disengagement Theory
--Activity Theory
--Disengagement or Activity?
Social Relationships in Late Adulthood
--Relationships with Children
--Relationships with Grandchildren
       --surrogate-parent role
       --fun-seeking grandparent role
       --grandparent-as-distant-figure role
       --parent-as-distant-figure role
       --reservoir-of-family-wisdom role
       --formal grandparenting style
--Relationships with Spouse
--Relationships with Friends
--Widowhood
Care of the Very Old
--Family Care
--Care Facilities for the Elderly
--Other Alternatives
Happiness in Old Age
       --Disengagement Theory
--Factors Linked to Happiness

Scrambles
Chapter 18

Scramble 1:   Listed below are Fisher's Five Periods of Older Adulthood. Match the 15 Characteristics with the Appropriate Stage.

Period		Characteristics		Points
A.	Continuity with Middle Age	1.	_____	_____
		2.	_____	_____
		3.	_____	_____
B.	Early Transition	1.	_____	_____
		2.	_____	_____
		3	._____	_____
C.	Revised Lifestyle	1.	_____	_____
		2.	_____	_____
		3.	_____	_____
D.	Later Transition	1.	_____	_____
		2.	_____	_____
		3.	_____	_____
E.	Final Period	1.	_____	_____
		2.	_____	_____
		3.	_____	_____

Your Total Points   _____
Total Possible Points   15
% =   _____

1.   Adaptation to changes of early transition
2.   Involuntary transitional events
3.   Loss of health and mobility
4.   Retirement plans pursued
5.   Adaptation to changes of later transition
6.   Socialization realized through age-group affiliations
7.   Middle-age lifestyle continued
8.   End of continuity with middle age
9.   Stable lifestyle appropriate to older adulthood
10.   Dependency
11.   Other activities substituted for work
12.   Voluntary transitional events
13.   Sense of finitude, mortality
14.   Need for assistance and/or care
15.   Loss of autonomy

Scramble 2: **Listed below are Atchley's 7 Phases of Retirement. Match the appropriate statement to fit the phase.**

Phase	Description	Points
Preretirement	_____	_____
Honeymoon	_____	_____
Rest and relaxation	_____	_____
Disenchantment	_____	_____
Reorientation	_____	_____
Routine	_____	_____
Termination	_____	_____

	Your Total Points	_____
	Total Possible Points	7
	% =	_____

1. Concern that retirement may not be as good as you thought it would
2. Settling down time
3. Reexamining life and what retirement is
4. Fantasies of what retirement will be like
5. Loss of independence
6. Intense and usually joyful activity
7. Establishing a routine

Scramble 3: **You remember Havighurst from several previous chapters. Without referring back to the Chapter (or Table 18.3) list 5 of his Developmental Tasks in Late Adulthood.**

Tasks	Points
1. _____	_____
2. _____	_____
3. _____	_____
4. _____	_____
5. _____	_____

Your Total Points	_____	
Total Possible Points	5	
% =	_____	

Scramble 4:   **Match the Appropriate Style of Grandparenting with the Appropriate Description.**

Roles of Grandparenting	Description	Points
1. Reservoir-of-family wisdom	_____	_____
2. Formal	_____	_____
3. Fun-seeking	_____	_____
4. Grandparent-as-distant	_____	_____
5. Surrogate-parent	_____	_____

	Your Total Points	_____
	Total Possible Points	5
	% =	_____

Scramble Summary

		Your Total Points	Possible Points
Scramble 1:	Fisher's Five Periods of Older Adulthood	_____	15
Scramble 2:	Atchley's Seven Phases of Retirement	_____	7
Scramble 3	Havighurst's Developmental Tasks	_____	5
Scramble 4:	Styles of Grandparenting	_____	5

	Your Total Points	_____
	Total Possible Points 32	
	% =	_____

III.   Experiencing

Main Points and Exercises

Exercises
Chapter 18

Views of Development in Late Adulthood

1.   Erikson's late adulthood stage, *integrity versus despair,* requires a positive evaluation of life and a decision that its final outcome is natural, inevitable, and acceptable. Peck details three psychosocial conflicts that compose the final Erikson stage: *ego differentiation versus work-role preoccupation* (need to shift preoccupations from career to self at retirement), *body transcendence versus body preoccupation* (danger of becoming preoccupied with declining physical and mental powers), and *ego transcendence versus ego preoccupation* (an acceptance of death).

Exercise 1:   List five people you know in late adulthood. Based on your interaction with them decide whether they have resolved the conflicts outlined by Erikson and Peck and the reasons for your decision. Put your response on a separate sheet.

Name   Integrity vs. Despair (Yes/No/Observations
1.

_____   Ego Differentiation - Work Role Preoccupation (Yes/No/Observations

_____   Body Transcendence-Body Preoccupation-(Yes/No/Observations

_____   Ego Transcendence-Ego Preoccupation-(Yes/No/Observations

Name   Integrity vs. Despair (Yes/No/Observations
2.

_____   Ego Differentiation - Work Role Preoccupation (Yes/No/Observations

_____   Body Transcendence-Body Preoccupation-(Yes/No/Observations

_____   Ego Transcendence-Ego Preoccupation-(Yes/No/Observations

Name   Integrity vs. Despair (Yes/No/Observations
3.

_____   Ego Differentiation - Work Role Preoccupation (Yes/No/Observations

_____   Body Transcendence-Body Preoccupation-(Yes/No/Observations

_____   Ego Transcendence-Ego Preoccupation-(Yes/No/Observations

Name _____ Integrity vs. Despair (Yes/No/Observations _____
4.

_____ Ego Differentiation - Work Role Preoccupation (Yes/No/Observations ____

_____ Body Transcendence-Body Preoccupation-(Yes/No/Observations ____

_____ Ego Transcendence-Ego Preoccupation-(Yes/No/Observations ____

Name _____ Integrity vs. Despair (Yes/No/Observations _____
5.

_____ Ego Differentiation - Work Role Preoccupation (Yes/No/Observations ____

_____ Body Transcendence-Body Preoccupation-(Yes/No/Observations ____

_____ Ego Transcendence-Ego Preoccupation-(Yes/No/Observations ____

2.	Fisher describes five stages in late adulthood; these stages exemplify stability following transitions: (1) continuity with middle age; (2) early transition; (3) revised lifestyle; (4) later transition; and (5) final period.

Exercise 2:	Following the same format as listed in Exercise 1 record your observations of the same individuals.

Name	Stage		Observations
1.	1.	Continuity with Middle	1.
			2.
			3.
	2.	Early Transition	1.
			2.
			3.
	3.	Revised Lifestyle	1.
			2.
			3.

204

	4.	Later Transition	1.
			2.
			3.
	5.	Final Period	1.
			2.
			3.

Name	Stage		Observations
2.	1.	Continuity with Middle	1.
			2.
			3.
	2.	Early Transition	1.
			2.
			3.
	3.	Revised Lifestyle	1.
			2.
			3.
	4.	Later Transition	1.
			2.
			3.
	5.	Final Period	1.
			2.
			3.

Name	Stage		Observations
3.	1.	Continuity with Middle	1.
			2.
			3.

	2.	Early Transition	1.
			2.
			3.
	3.	Revised Lifestyle	1.
			2.
			3.
	4.	Later Transition	1.
			2.
			3.
	5.	Final Period	1.
			2.
			3.

Name	Stage		Observations
4.	1.	Continuity with Middle	1.
			2.
			3.
	2.	Early Transition	1.
			2.
			3.
	3.	Revised Lifestyle	1.
			2.
			3.
	4.	Later Transition	1.
			2.
			3.
	5.	Final Period	1.
			2.
			3.

Name	Stage		Observations
5.	1.	Continuity with Middle	1.
			2.
			3.
	2.	Early Transition	1.
			2.
			3.
	3.	Revised Lifestyle	1.
			2.
			3.
	4.	Later Transition	1.
			2.
			3.
	5.	Final Period	1.
			2.
			3.

The Life Review

3.   Personal narratives are sensible stories of our lives that give them continuity and purpose. The life review is an active process wherein the personal narrative of the older adult involves reminiscing, evaluating, resolving old conflicts, and coming to terms with the finality of life.

Exercise 3a: Here is an opportunity that you would not ordinarily take until you were into late adulthood but because of the Lifespan Development course you can exercise now. You can develop your personal narrative on life review to this point in your life. Following the ideas in the book what are your life's themes, behaviors that stand out, how do you understand yourself and other because of it?

Exercise 3b: What has been the main theme, the life reviews of your mother and father grandmother and grandfather? Does it sound similar to your own? Has this exercise helped you to understand your families themes?

Retirement

4.   Retirement is a 20th-century phenomenon made possible by a high standard of living, high worker productivity, and a surplus of labor. Attitudes toward retirement are important predictors of satisfaction and healthy adjustment after retirement. Retirement is most likely to be positive if it is voluntary rather than forced, if work is not the only thing in the person's life, if health and income are sufficient to permit the enjoyment of newly created leisure time, and if retirement has been planned.

Exercise 4a: Did your grandparents (or even parents) handle retirement smoothly or was it descriptive? How do they view it presently?

Exercise 4b: Considering what you have read about retirement - How do you view your own? Will you make any adjustments in your own thinking about retirement as a result of what you have read? If so -- what?

5.   Atchley describes several phases of retirement: *preretirement* (fantasies about retirement), *honeymoon* (vigorous doing of things not done before), *rest and relaxation* (a quiet period, *disenchantment* (a relatively rare period of disillusionment), *reorientation* (coming to terms with disenchantment, *routine* (establishing satisfying routines), and *termination* (withdrawal from the retirement role).

Exercise 5a: You have been asked to give a five minute speech on retirement to a group of potentially new retirees. How would you summarize Atchley's seven phases so as to make it meaningful for someone who is about to make this big decision?

Exercise 5b: Discuss with someone who has retired (your parents, grandparents, relative or other) Atchley's phases. What phase do they feel they are in? Do they agree with the phases? What are your own observations?

Successful Aging

6. Most of the elderly cope with the processes of aging and continue to find contentment and joy in their lives. Disengagement theory suggests that, with failing physical and mental capabilities, the elderly seek to withdraw from active social roles and that they should be allowed, perhaps encouraged, to do so. Activity theory argues that continued social, physical, and emotional involvement is important to physical and emotional well-being.

Exercise 6: List five people you know who have retired (list couples if you wish). Based on your observation are they adhering to the disengagement or activity theory? Put down your observations as justification.

Retired Person(s)	Disengaged or Active	Observation
1.		
2.		
3.		
4.		
5.		

Social Relationships in Late Adulthood

7. Family relationships are ordinarily the most important of all social relationships throughout the entire lifespan--and other than that with a spouse, the most important are with children. Grandparents can play different roles: surrogate parent (caring for children), fun-seeking (indulgent playmate), distant figure (occasional gifts),m reservoir-of-family-wisdom (patriarch or matriarch of extended family), and formal nonintrusive but emotionally involved).

Exercise 7a: Which of the five different styles of grandparenting was exercised from your mother's side? On what do you base your observation? Which style on your father's side? On what do you base your observation?

Exercise 7b: Listed below are the five different styles of grandparenting. Name a couple you know practicing each (ask among your friends how their grandparents react to them. On what do you (or your friends) base your observations?

Style	Name	Observations	(Specific Behaviors)
	1.		
Formal			
Fun Seeking			

Style	Name	Observations	(Specific Behaviors)
	2.		
Formal			
Fun Seeking			

Style	Name	Observations	(Specific Behaviors)
	3.		
Formal			
Fun Seeking			

Style	Name	Observations	(Specific Behaviors)
	4.		
Formal			
Fun Seeking			

Style	Name	Observations	(Specific Behaviors)
	5.		
Formal			
Fun Seeking			

8. Marriages tend to become happier with the empty nest and remain happy and sexually active into old age. Among women, decline in sexual activity is most often due to lack of a suitable partner. In late adulthood, close friends serve important roles relating to intimacy, social and intellectual stimulation, confiding, relieving stress, and providing support during crises.

Care of the Very Old

9.   Filial responsibility is a common feature of most family systems, often evident in children caring for their aging parents. A small percentage of the very old, often as a last resort or for medical reasons, are in special care facilities like nursing homes. Increasing numbers also live in communities designed for the elderly. Various forms of community-based assistance sometimes make it possible for the somewhat-dependent elderly to continue to live in their homes with relative independence.

Happiness in Old Age

10.   Both disengagement and continued activity may be associated with happiness or unhappiness. Health, income, friendships, and personality variables appear to be important factors for happiness in late adulthood.

I.   **Reading and Understanding**

Dying
Chapter 19

This Chapter
Death
--Some Definitions
        --death
        --bereavement
        --grief
        --mourning
Notions of Death Through the Lifespan
--Distancing and Denying Death
--Children's Understanding of Death
--Adolescent Notions of Death
--Notions of Death in Early and Middle Adulthood
--Views of Death in Late Adulthood
        --Fear of Dying
        --Ego Integrity
Dying
--Stages of Dying
--Life's Trajectories
        --Dying Trajectories
                --dying trajectory
                --expected swift death
                --expected temporary recovery
                --expected lingering while dying
        --Reactions to Knowledge of Imminent Dying
                --terminal phase
--Terminal Care
        --Palliative Care and Hospices
--Euthanasia
        --Definitions
                --active euthanasia
                --passive euthanasia
        --The Controversy
        --The Living Will
Bereavement and Grieving
        --bereavement
        --grief
        --mourning
--Effects of Bereavement
        --Short-Term Effects
        --Long-Term Effects
        --Anticipatory Grief
Final Themes
        --Development is continuous
        --Maturity is relative
        --Development is contextual
        --Developmental influences are bidirectional
        --Heredity and environment interact throughout the lifespan
        --There is no average person

## II.	Learning and Comprehending

Scrambles
Chapter 19

Scramble 1:	Your book lists seven reasons for being afraid to die. Without referring to your book see if you can list five:

Reasons to Fear Dying	Points
1.	_____
2.	_____
3.	_____
4.	_____
5.	_____

Your Total Points _____

Total Possible Points   5

% = _____

Scramble 2:	Scrambled below are both the stages and statements of Kubler-Ross. Put the stages in the appropriate sequence along with the proper statement.

Stage	Statement	Points
Bargaining	_____	_____
Acceptance	_____	_____
Anger	_____	_____
Denial	_____	_____
Depression	_____	_____

Your Total Points _____

Total Possible Points   10

% = _____

1.	"Let it happen. It's okay. I'm not interested in anything anymore. I'm not happy, just tired."
2.	"Why me? Lots of people smoked more than I did, and look at them! It isn't fair!"
3.	"Okay, I might die. Just let me live a little longer so I can wrap up the business and see my new grandson."
4.	"Not me! I don't believe it! There must be a mistake!"
5.	"Yes, it's happening. There's nothing I can do. I wish I had died a long time ago."

Scramble 3: Scrambled below are the Common Causes of Death. Without referring to Figure 19.2 separately rank the causes for males and females. Note the differences. Were you surprised at these differences? How would you explain them?

Common Causes of Death	Female Ranking	Male Ranking	Points
1. Pneumonia, flu	_____	_____	_____
2. Accidents and Adverse Effects	_____	_____	_____
3. Malignant Neoplasms	_____	_____	_____
4. Suicide	_____	_____	_____
5. Cerebrovascular Disease	_____	_____	_____
6. Diabetes Mellitus	_____	_____	_____
7. Heart Disease	_____	_____	_____
8. Pulmonary Disease	_____	_____	_____
9. Homicide and Legal Intervention	_____	_____	_____
10. Liver Disease	_____	_____	_____

Your Total Points   _____

Total Possible Points   20

% =   _____

Scramble Summary

Scramble 1: Reasons for Being Afraid to Died   _____

Scramble 2: Kubler-Ross - Stages of Death and Dying   _____

Scramble 3: Male-Female Common Causes of Death   _____

Your Total Score   _____

Total Possible Points   35

% =   _____

Main Points and Exercises

Exercises
Chapter 19

Death

1.   Neurological, or brain, death signifies cessation of electrical activity in the brain. *Bereavement* describes a loss; *grief* is an intense emotional reaction to bereavement; and *mourning* describes the things people do when they are grieving.

Exercise 1:   Has someone you have known died? Relate the following terms to the death and the reactions of others.

Bereavement

Grief

Mourning

Notions of Death Through the Lifespan

2.   Our culture tends to distance and deny death (through euphemisms and avoidance of contact or care). Very young children often do not completely understand the finality of death, although media exposure has made them considerably more sophisticated. With advancing age, declining health and other events conspire to make us more conscious of our mortality. Fear of death appears at all stages of life.

Exercise 2:   Why do you fear death (assuming you do). Now talk to ten of your friends and ask each why they might fear death. Do any of them fear it the same way you do? Is there a consensus? Were there any reasons other than the seven listed in the book? What was your friend's attitude about asking this question?

Dying

3.   Kubler-Ross describes five possible stages of dying (for those who know death is imminent: *denial* ("not me"), *anger* ("why me?"), *bargaining* ("let me suffer less and I will..."), *depression*, and *acceptance*. Not all people go through these stages and in this order.

Exercise 3: Try to recall someone close to you who has died. (If you have not had this experience ask your parents or friends to assist you.) Go through Kubler-Ross's five possible stages and try to determine statements they made that reflect each stage. If you have had someone close to you die recently recall statements you or others may have made (on the dying individual) that reflects those stages.

4. Our life trajectories are our expected spans of life. When something happens to inform us that our trajectories will end, our perspectives change from life trajectory to dying trajectory. Medically, the phrase *dying trajectory* refers to the speed with which a person is expected to die.

Exercise 4: Your friend Morbid is interested in death and dying. Briefly outline how you would tell him about Kubler-Ross's stages and the life trajectory theory. How would you clarify differences and similarities? How would Pattison's three phases of personal trajectory? Explain the medical term "dying trajectory".

5. *Pulliative care* for the terminally ill is designed to ease their dying as well as to make things easier for the bereaved. *Hospice care* is short-term care for the terminally ill outside a hospital setting, sometimes in the patient's home or in centers designed specifically for that purpose.

Exercise 5a: Assume that you are totally responsible for an elderly person who has been diagnosed as terminally ill. Would you consider palliative care or hospice care? How would you feel about selecting such care?

Exercise 5b: Imagine yourself in the position of being terminally ill. Would you wish to have palliative or hospice care?

Exercise 5c: List three advantages of palliative or hospice care. List three disadvantages of such care.

6.   *Euthanasia,* popularly called *mercy killing*, is a controversial procedure that can be either passive (not doing something that would prolong life) or active (deliberately doing something to shorten life). Under certain conditions, it is completely legal in Holland.

Exercise 6a: Do you believe in euthanasia? To be more objective listed below are sections for three arguments for and three arguments against euthanasia.

Arguments for Euthanasia   Arguments Against Euthanasia

1.   1.

2.   2.

3.   3.

Exercise 6b: Would you, your parents or grandparents be willing sign a living will? Could you discuss it with your family? What would be their response? Could you discuss the living will as presented on Figure 19.4 in your book?

Bereavement and Grieving

7.   Grief can result in a wide range of short-term symptoms and behaviors (appetite loss, sleep disturbances, crying); longer-term effects of bereavement can include psychological and physical problems, sometimes evident in serious depression. For some, experiencing grief (grief work) may be important for mental and psychological well-being. Sometimes *anticipatory grief* (profound grief that results when the bereaved first learns about the impending death) may reduce the length and severity of subsequent grieving.

Exercise 7:   Recall the death that you were most closely associated with. What form of bereavement, grief, and mourning did you experience? What forms did you observe in others? Is there a family reaction to a relative dying?

Final Themes

8.   Development is continuous from birth until death. Maturity is always relative rather than absolute. At all stages, context exerts a profound, bidirectional influence on the person. Nature and nurture interaction throughout life. Ultimately, there is no average person.

Exercise 8:   Listed below are the six themes defining the lifespan perspective. Write a sentence or two to express your impression of these themes.

Development is Continuous:

Maturity Is Relative:

Development is Contextual:

Development Influences are Bidirectional:

Heredity and Environment Interacts Throughout the Lifespan:

There is no Average Person:

9.   There are always new roses.

Exercise 9:   In one hundred years a distant relative passes through a cemetery and sees your tombstone. They see -- Here Lies _____. Underneath your name is you _____. It reads. "....."

Finale

And now your lifespan journey is complete. Hopefully it was as successful as you hoped it would be. All journeys take twists into areas we did not know existed as well as into areas that provide a pleasant surprise. I suspect this journey was no different for you. Hopefully the study guide was helpful taking you places you never thought you would go and broadening your horizons.

Although the material here will be for the most part forgotten, it can always be used as a reference source and long after your college days are over you will find yourself saying "Oh yes -- I learned that in a lifespan course I had." If you have planned well the exercises will be there at your finger tips or more hopefully at the tip of your tongue.

It was the intent of the study guide to help you become successful on your lifespan journey not just in attaining an acceptable grade but in your personal growth as well.

If the student resource guide helped you develop more questions than answers, provided insight into your friends and family as well as your own life it has served its purpose. In any case the journey will continue.

Psychology Ch 1	Developmental Psychology Ch 1
Lifespan Developmental Psychology Ch 1	Ecology Ch 1
Bidirectional Ch 1	Oral Rehydration Therapy (ORT) Ch 1
Baby Tossing Ch 1	Nonnaturalistic Observation Ch 1

Experiment Ch 1	Variables Ch 1
Independent Variable Ch 1	Dependent Variable Ch 1
Hypothesis Ch 1	Experimental Groups Ch 1
Control Groups Ch 1	Correlational Studies Ch 1

Retrospective Studies <div align="right">Ch 1</div>	Longitudinal Study <div align="right">Ch 1</div>
Cross-sectional Study <div align="right">Ch 1</div>	Cohort <div align="right">Ch 1</div>
Sequential Designs <div align="right">Ch 1</div>	Time Lag Study <div align="right">Ch 1</div>
Generalizability <div align="right">Ch 1</div>	Sampling <div align="right">Ch 1</div>

Ecological (cross-culture) Validity Ch 1	Experimenter Bias Ch 1
Double Blind Procedure Ch 1	Subject Bias Ch 1
Hawthorne Effect Ch 1	The Mythical Average Ch 1
tabula rasa Ch 1	 Ch 1

Four Aspects of the Lifespan View Ch 1	Three Important Concepts in the Study of the Lifespan Ch 1
Six Snapshots of Child Rearing Ch 1	Children's Rights Today Ch 1
List 2 Early Pioneers and Their Position Regarding Children Ch 1	List 2 Later Pioneers and Their Position Regarding Children Ch 1
Methods of Study Lifespan Development Ch 1	Four Types of Naturalistic Observation Ch 1

Diary Description Ch 1	Specimen Description Ch 1
Event Sampling Ch 1	Time Sampling Ch 1
Two Types of Nonnaturalistic Observation Ch 1	List Some Special Lifespan Research Problems Ch 1
What are the Items Used in the Checklist for Evaluting Developmental Research? Ch 1	 Ch 1

Nominal Fallacy Ch 2	Theory Ch 2
Heuristic Value Ch 2	Organismic Model (active) Ch 2
Mechanistic Model (reactive) Ch 2	Contextual (Ecological) Model Ch 2
Libido Ch 2	Id Ch 2

Reflexes Ch 2	Psychic Energy Ch 2
Ego Ch 2	Superego Ch 2
Conscience Ch 2	Identity Ch 2
Psychosexual Stages Ch 2	Oral Stage Ch 2

Anal Period Ch 2	Phallic Stage Ch 2
Oedipus Complex Ch 2	Electra Complex Ch 2
Sexual Latency Ch 2	Identification Ch 2
Genital Stage Ch 2	Defense Mechanism Ch 2

Displacement Ch 2	Reaction Formation Ch 2
Intellectualization Ch 2	Projection Ch 2
Denial Ch 2	Repression Ch 2
Identity Ch 2	Psychosocial Stages Ch 2

Ego Identity Ch 2	Identity Diffusion Ch 2
Developmental Tasks Ch 2	Behaviorism Ch 2
Classical Conditioning Ch 2	Unconditioned Stimulus (US) Ch 2
Conditioned Stimulus (CS) Ch 2	Unconditioned Response (UR) Ch 2

Conditioned Emotional Reaction (CER) Ch 2	Elicited Ch 2
Emitted Ch 2	Operant Ch 2
Respondent Ch 2	Operant Conditioning Ch 2
Consequences Ch 2	Reinforcement Ch 2

Reinforcer Ch 2	Positive Reinforcement Ch 2
Negative Reinforcement Ch 2	Reward Ch 2
Relief Ch 2	Punishment Ch 2
Castigation Ch 2	Penalty Ch 2

Behavior Modification Ch 2	Cognitive Theory Ch 2
Observational Learning (Imitation) Ch 2	Model Ch 2
Symbolic Ch 2	The Modeling Effect Ch 2
The Inhibitory-Disinhibitory Effect Ch 2	The Eliciting Effect Ch 2

Self=efficacy Ch 2	Self-referent Ch 2
Assimilation Ch 2	Accommodation Ch 2
Adaptation Ch 2	Scheme (schemata) (schemato) Ch 2
Sensorimotor Period Ch 2	Preoperational Thinking Ch 2

Concrete Operations Ch 2	Formal Operations Ch 2
Ethology (ethologists) Ch 2	Imprinting Ch 2
Critical Period Ch 2	Releaser Ch 2
Sensitive Period Ch 2	Zone of Proximal Development Ch 2

Social Speech Ch 2	Egocentric Speech Ch 2
Inner Speech Ch 2	Open Systems Ch 2
Microsystem Ch 2	Mesosystem Ch 2
Exosystem Ch 2	Macrosystem Ch 2

List Characteristics of a Good Theory Ch 2	Three Levels of Personality (Freud) Ch 2
List 6 Defense mechanisms Ch 2	Havighurst's Theory Ch 2
2 Assumptions of Behaviorism Ch 2	2 Early Pioneers Ch 2
Four Basic Elements of Classical Conditioning Ch 2	2 Kinds of Punishment Ch 2

Bandura's Theory Ch 2	Implications of Self-Efficacy Judgment Ch 2
Piaget's Four Stages of Cognitive Development Ch 2	Vygotsky's Basic Ideas Ch 2
Three Basic Themes Underlying Vygotsky's Theory Ch 2	Bronfenbrenner's Basic Principle Ch 2
Ecological Systems Theory Ch 2	The 4 Systems Devised by Bronfenbrenner Ch 2

Maslow's Theory

Ch 2

Ch 2

Ch 2

Ch 2

Ch 2

Ch 2

Ch 2

Ch 2

Feral Children Ch 3	Addictive (heredity-environment) Ch 3
Interactive (heredity-environment) Ch 3	Conception Ch 3
Ovum (egg cell) Ch 3	Sperm Cell Ch 3
Artificial Insemination Ch 3	In Vitro Ch 3

Sex Cells Ch 3	Puberty Ch 3
Menopause Ch 3	Menstrual Cycle Ch 3
Gametes Ch 3	Genetics Ch 3
Proteins Ch 3	DNA (deoxyribonnucleic acid) Ch 3

Double Helix Ch 3	Chromosomes Ch 3
Mitosis Ch 3	Mature Sex Cells Ch 3
Meiosis Ch 3	Sex Chromosomes Ch 3
Autosomes Ch 3	Genes Ch 3

Dominant Gene Ch 3	Recessive Gene Ch 3
Mutations Ch 3	Genotype Ch 3
Phenotype Ch 3	Reaction Range Ch 3
Canalization Epigenetic Landscape Ch 3	Epigenesis Ch 3

Mendelion Genetics Ch 3	Molecular Genetics Ch 3
RFLSs (Restriction Fragment Length Polymorphisms) Ch 3	Marker Genes Ch 3
Genome Ch 3	Hemophilia Ch 3
Sickle-Cell Anemia Ch 3	Heterogygous Ch 3

Homogygous Ch 3	PKU (Phenylketonuria) Ch 3
Tay-Sachs Disease Ch 3	Muscular-Dystropy (MD) Ch 3
Neural Tube Defects Ch 3	Spina Bifida Ch 3
Anencephaly Ch 3	AFP Test Ch 3

Alphafetoprotein Ch 3	Diabetes Mellitus Ch 3
Chromosomal Disorders Ch 3	Down Syndrome Ch 3
Tresomy 21 Ch 3	XYY Males Ch 3
Fragile X Syndrome Ch 3	Amniocentesis Ch 3

Amniotic Fluid Ch 3	Chorionic Villus Biopsy (CVS) Ch 3
Vetra Sound Ch 3	Fetoscopy Ch 3
Radiography Ch 3	Preimplanation Diagnosis Ch 3
Monozygotic (identical) Twins Ch 3	Dizygotic (fraternal) Twins Ch 3

Rubber Band Hypothesis

Ch 3

Ch 3

Ch 3

Ch 3

Ch 3

Ch 3

Ch 3

Ch 3

Two Models of Gender-Context Relationships Ch 3	Plomin-relationship Between Genotype and Phenotype Ch 3
List 3 Major Genetic Defects Ch 3	Huntington Disease (Huntington's Chorea) Ch 3
List 4 Additional Genetic Defects Ch 3	List 5 Nonmedical Conditions That May Be Linked to Genetic Defects Ch 3
List 4 Abnormalities of Sex Chromosomes Ch 3	Turner's Syndrome Ch 3

Klinefelter's Syndrome Ch 3	Sex Techniques for Fetal Diagnosis Ch 3
Galton's Conclusion Ch 3	Sherman and Key Study (Mountain Children) Ch 3
   Ch 3	 Ch 3
   Ch 3	 Ch 3

Menses Ch 4	Quickening Ch 4
Gestation Period Ch 4	Zygote Ch 4
Germinal Stage Ch 4	Embryo Stage Ch 4
Fetus Stage Ch 4	Fertilization Ch 4

Fallopian Tubes Ch 4	Ovaries Ch 4
Uterus Ch 4	Villi Ch 4
Placenta Ch 4	In Utero Ch 4
Genitalia Ch 4	Babinski Reflex Ch 4

Lanugo Ch 4	Proximodistal Ch 4
Cephalocaudal Ch 4	Teratogens Ch 4
Mutagens Ch 4	Teras Ch 4
Cytomegalovirus Ch 4	Thalidomide Ch 4

Quinine Ch 4	Barbiturates Ch 4
Anesthetics Ch 4	DES - Diethylstibestrol Ch 4
Endocrine Disrupting Ch 4	Methylmercury Ch 4
Minimata Disease Ch 4	PCB's (polychlorinated: biphenyls) Ch 4

Dioxin Ch 4	Methyl Isocyanate Ch 4
Lead Effects Ch 4	Fetal Alcohol Syndrome (FAS) Ch 4
Fetal Alcohol Effects Ch 4	Neonatal Abstinence Syndrome Ch 4
Methadone Maintenance Ch 4	Bounder Babies Ch 4

Rubella Ch 4	Herpes Simplex 2 Ch 4
Amenorrhea Ch 4	Rh Factor Ch 4
"D" Ch 4	Rh (D) Immunization Ch 4
Fetal Crythroblastosis Ch 4	Transplacental Hemorrhage Ch 4

Rhlg-Rhogam Immune Globulin Ch 4	Labor Ch 4
Abortion (Miscarriage) Ch 4	Immature Birth Ch 4
Premature Birth Ch 4	Mature Birth Ch 4
Postmature Birth Ch 4	SGA Small for Gestational Age Ch 4

LGA Large for Gestational Age Ch 4	AGA Average for Gestational Age Ch 4
Cervix Ch 4	Amniotic Sac Ch 4
Episiotomy Ch 4	Breech Ch 4
Transverse Ch 4	Version Ch 4

Neonate Ch 4	D & C: Dilation-Curettage Ch 4
Cesarean Delivery Ch 4	Epiderman Analygesia Ch 4
Natural Childbirth (prepared childbirth) Ch 4	Midwife Ch 4
Postpartum Depression Ch 4	Forceps Ch 4

Anoxia Ch 4	Prolapsed Cord Ch 4
Incubators (isolettes) Ch 4	TPN Total Parenteral Nutrition Ch 4
      Ch 4	 Ch 4
      Ch 4	 Ch 4

Four Factors in Detecting Pregnancy Ch 4	List the Three Stages of Prenatal Development Ch 4
List 3 Factors That Can Affect Prenatal Development Ch 4	Factors Influencing Teratogens Effects Ch 4
Effects of Nicotine Ch 4	Effects of Caffeine Ch 4
Effects of Narcotics Ch 4	Effects of Marijuana Ch 4

Effects of Cocaine Ch 4	List l0 Symptoms of Children Born to ????? Addicted Mothers Ch 4
List 7 Diseases a Pregnant Mother May Have That Will Affect a Child Ch 4	Effects of Diabetes Ch 4
Effects of Herpes Ch 4	Effects of Acquired Immunity Defense Syndrome Ch 4
Effects of Older Mothers on Children Ch 4	List 7 Symptoms in Children of Teenage Mothers Ch 4

List the 5 Classifications of Birth (Gestation) Ch 4	Grant: Three Ways of Solving Problems of Maternal Death Ch 4
List the Three Classifications by Weight and Gestation Ch 4	List the Three Stages of Birth Ch 4
Stage One: Dilation Ch 4	Stage Two: Delivery Ch 4
Stage Three: Afterbirth Ch 4	Apgar Scale (List 5 Different Measures) Ch 4

Brazelton Neonatal Behavioral Assessment Scale (NBAS) Ch 4	Dick- Read Process Ch 4
Lamaze Method Ch 4	LeBoyer Method Ch 4
List 5 Factors Involved in Prematurity Ch 4	List 3 Levels of Birthweight (list weight) Used in Infant Research Ch 4
List 5 Effects of Prematurity Ch 4	 Ch 4

Infans Ch 5	Neonate Ch 5
Breast Feeding Statistics Ch 5	Bottle Feeding Statistics Ch 5
Diarrhea Ch 5	Genital Growth Ch 5
Pubescence Ch 5	Lymphoid Growth Ch 5

Neural Development Ch 5	Cretinism Ch 5
Sudden Infant Death Syndrome (SIDS) Ch 5	Apnea Ch 5
The Orienting Response Ch 5	Galvanic Skin Response (GSR)-Electro Thermal Response Ch 5
Habituation Ch 5	Sucking Reflex Ch 5

Vegetative Reflex Ch 5	Head Turning Reflex (Rooting Reflex) Ch 5
Moro Reflex Ch 5	Equilibration Ch 5
Here and Now World Ch 5	Object Concept Ch 5
Object Permanence Ch 5	Sensorimotor Development Ch 5

Exercising Reflexes Ch 5	Primary Circular Reactions Ch 5
Secondard Circular Reactions Ch 5	Purposeful Coordinations Ch 5
Intention Ch 5	Tertiary Circular Action Ch 5
Mental Representation Ch 5	Imitation Ch 5

Deferred Imitation Ch 5	Language Ch 5
Psycholinguistics Ch 5	Elements of Language Ch 5
Phonology Ch 5	Phonemes Ch 5
Morphemes Ch 5	Semantics (Meaning) Ch 5

Syntax (Grammar) Ch 5	Pragmatics Ch 5
Active Vocabulary Ch 5	Passive Vocabulary Ch 5
Prespeech Stage Ch 5	Speech Stage Ch 5
Symbols Ch 5	Simple Representation Ch 5

Symbolic Representation Ch 5	(LASS) Language Acquisition Support System Ch 5
Sound Discrimination Ch 5	Melodic Sounds Ch 5
Vocalic Sounds Ch 5	Emotional Sounds Ch 5
Babbling Ch 5	The First Word Ch 5

Sentencelike Words (Holophrase) Ch 5	Multiword Stage Ch 5
Telegraphic Speech Ch 5	 Ch 5
   Ch 5	 Ch 5
   Ch 5	 Ch 5

5 Common - 4 Different Aspects of Human Growth Ch 5	Effects of Severe Malnutrition on Neural Development Ch 5
List 3 Common Characteristics of SIDS Ch 5	Triple Risk Model (Conditions) Ch 5
Three Areas of Perceptual Development Ch 5	Three Measures Used in Studying Infant Memory Ch 5
Developmental Phases in Infant Memory (Describe Each) Ch 5	Adult Strategies to Remember Ch 5

2 Year Old Strategies to Remember Ch 5	Six Stages of Sensorimotor Development Ch 5
Piaget's 4 Stages of Cognitive Development Ch 5	Hay, Stinson and Castle-Three Types of Learning That Imitation Makes Possible Ch 5
Three Essential Characteristics of Language Ch 5	Three Different Behaviors of Prespeech Stage Ch 5
Two Critical Achievements in Prespeech Period Ch 5	Two Kinds of Representation Ch 5

Three Kinds of Infant Sounds Ch 5	Six Sequential Stages of Learning a Language Ch 5
Masur's Three Widely Reocgnized General-Learning Milestones Ch 5	 Ch 5
     Ch 5	 Ch 5
     Ch 5	 Ch 5

Sanguine Ch 6	Phlegmatic Ch 6
Choleric Ch 6	Melancholic Ch 6
Ecology Ch 6	Macrosystems Ch 6
Temperament Ch 6	Dyadic Ch 6

"Second Order" Effects Ch 6	Infant States Ch 6
Rapid Eye Movements (REM) Sleep Ch 6	Personality Ch 6
Trait Ch 6	Types Ch 6
NYLS-New York Longitudinal Study Ch 6	Difficult Infants Ch 6

Easy Infants Ch 6	Slow-To-Warm-Up Infants Ch 6
Early Infancy Temperament Questionnaire Ch 6	Revised Infant Temperament Questionnaire Ch 6
EAS Approach Ch 6	Goodness-of-Fit Ch 6
Brow Bulge Ch 6	Nasolabial Furrow Ch 6

Amencephalic Ch 6	Gewirtz-3 Stages in the Development of Smiling Behavior Ch 6
Incongruence Ch 6	Self-Directed and Other-Directed Regulatory Behaviors Ch 6
Mother Deprived Monkeys Ch 6	Strange Situation (Ainworth) Ch 6
Securely Attached Ch 6	Insecurely Attached (Anxious Avoidant) Ch 6

Insecure Avoidant (Anxious Avoidant) Ch 6	Insecure Ambivalent Ch 6
Disorganized-Disoriented (Unclassified) Ch 6	Attachment Ch 6
Mother-Infant Bonding Ch 6	Ethnologists Ch 6
Critical Period Ch 6	Growth Failure or Failure to Thrive (FTT) or Maternal Deprivation Syndrome Ch 6

Preadaptations Ch 6	Cyclical Motor Movements Ch 6
Preattachment Ch 6	Attachment in the Making Ch 6
Clear Cut Attachment Ch 6	Goal-Connected Attachment Ch 6
Goal-Connected Attachment Ch 6	Affiliative Behaviors Ch 6

Separation Protest Ch 6	Freezing Ch 6
Mutism Ch 6	Incongruity Hypothesis (Hebb) Ch 6
Multiple Caregiving Ch 6	Cortisol Ch 6
Transitional Objects (Security Blankets) Ch 6	Individuation Ch 6

Infant Care Ch 6	Insecure-Secure Attachment Ch 6
Two Conclusions of Studies of Mother-Infant Studies and Infant Care Ch 6	Quality of Day Care Ch 6
Gender Roles (Sex Roles) Ch 6	Gender Typing Ch 6
Developmental Delays Ch 6	Cerebral Palsy (Significant Developmental Motor Disability) Ch 6

Little's Disease Ch 6	Congenital Disorder Ch 6
Anorexia Ch 6	Spasticity Ch 6
Dyskinesia Ch 6	Orofacial Proxes Ch 6
Developmental Coordination Disorder Ch 6	Epilepsy Ch 6

Grand Mal Seizure Ch 6	Petit Mal Seizure Ch 6
Benign Infantile Epilepsy Ch 6	Autism Ch 6
Pervasive Developmental Disorder Ch 6	 Ch 6
   Ch 6	 Ch 6

Two Ways The Contextual Model Differs From the Dyadic Model Ch 6	Wolf-6 Distinct Infant States Ch 6
List 9 Temperament Characteristics of Infants Ch 6	Three Emotions Outlined by Watson Ch 6
Four Types of Infant Cries Ch 6	Four Categories of Attachment Ch 6
Bowlby's Four Phases in the Infant's Development of Attachment Ch 6	List 3 Types of Separation Studies Ch 6

Six Important Dimensions of Parenting Ch 6	Three Symptoms of Autism Ch 6
   Ch 6	 Ch 6
   Ch 6	 Ch 6
   Ch 6	 Ch 6

Ratio of Head to Body Size Ch 7	Preschooler's Health Problems Ch 7
Denver Developmental Screening Test (Denver II) Ch 7	Developmentally Delayed Ch 7
Iron Deficient Infants Ch 7	Motor Skills and Intelligence Ch 7
Goodenough Draw-a-Man Ch 7	Goodenough-Harris Drawing Test Ch 7

Draw-A-Person Test Ch 7	Motor Development and Social Development Ch 7
Infantile Amnesia Ch 7	Incidental Mnemonics Ch 7
Wellman (2 Things Important About Preschooler's Primitive Memory Strategies) Ch 7	Metamemory Ch 7
Sensorimotor Intelligence Ch 7	Preoperational Ch 7

Operation Ch 7	Reversibility Ch 7
Undoing Ch 7	Preconceptual Ch 7
Intuitive Ch 7	Preconceptual Thinking Ch 7
Concepts Ch 7	Preconcepts Ch 7

Deduction Ch 7	Induction Ch 7
Transductive Reasoning Ch 7	Syncretic Reasoning Ch 7
Intuitive Thinking Ch 7	Egocentric Thought Ch 7
Conservation Ch 7	Number Concepts Ch 7

Number Abstraction Skills Ch 7	Minimal Reasoning Principles Ch 7
Preschool Education Ch 7	Nursery Schools Ch 7
Educare Ch 7	Compensatory Preschool Programs Ch 7
Project Head Start Ch 7	Life Success Measures Ch 7

Family as a Child Rearing Unit Ch 7	Preschool Intervention - "Model" Approaches Ch 7
Montessori Method Ch 7	Kindergartens Ch 7
Miseducating Ch 7	"Gold Medal" Parents Ch 7
Fear of Failure Ch 7	"College Degree" Parents Ch 7

Language Ch 7	Comprehension Ch 7
American Sign Language Ch 7	Sign Speaking Ch 7
Duos Ch 7	Multiple Word Sentences Ch 7
Morphemes Ch 7	Conjunction Ch 7

Embedding Ch 7	Permutation Ch 7
Chomsky Ch 7	Critical Period Based Ch 7
Language Acquisition Device (LAD) Ch 7	Child Directed Language (Motherese) Ch 7
Bilingualism Ch 7	Two Views on Psychological Effect of Bilingualism Ch 7

Subtractive Bilingualism Ch 7	Additive Bilingualism Ch 7
Transitional Bilingualism Ch 7	Balanced Bilinguals Ch 7
English Only Ch 7	English Plus Ch 7
Speech and Language Problems Ch 7	Whorfian Ch 7

Four Areas Examined by the Denver Developmental Screening Test Ch 7	Three Activities Important to Memory Strategies Ch 7
Five Stages in Early Development of Memory Strategies Ch 7	Two Subperiods of the Preoperational Period Ch 7
Two Main Types of Logical Reasoning Ch 7	Two Principal Classes of Explanations for the Development of Language Ch 7
Three Reasons for Subtractive Bilingualism Ch 7	Two Forms of the Whorfian Hypothesis Ch 7

Socialization (Social Learning) Ch 8	Erikson's Psychosocial Stages Ch 8
Psychosocial Development Ch 8	Trust Versus Mistrust Ch 8
Autonomy Versus Shame and Doubt Ch 8	Intentionality Ch 8
Initiative Versus Guilt Ch 8	Autonomous Self Ch 8

Imitation Ch 8	Identification Ch 8
Modeling Effect Ch 8	Inhibitory and Disinhibitory Effects Ch 8
Eliciting Effect Ch 8	4-Person Cooperation Board Ch 8
Cooperation Vs. Competition Ch 8	The Imbonggu Kila-Kila Study Ch 8

Symbolic Models Ch 8	Social Referencing Ch 8
Self-Directed Regulatory Behavior Ch 8	Other-Directed Regulatory Behavior Ch 8
Display Rules Ch 8	Play Ch 8
Practice Play (Sensorimotor Play) Ch 8	Imaginative Play Ch 8

Pretend Play Ch 8	Daydreaming Ch 8
Theory of Mind Ch 8	Metacognition Ch 8
Social Play Ch 8	Solitary Play Ch 8
Primitive Social Play Ch 8	Onlooker Play Ch 8

Parallel Play Ch 8	Associative Play Ch 8
Cooperative Play Ch 8	Gender Roles Ch 8
Gender Typing Ch 8	Gender Schemas (Gender Scripts) Ch 8
Introjection Ch 8	Basic Gender Identity Ch 8

Gender Stability Ch 8	Gender Consistency Ch 8
Stereotypes Ch 8	Sex Differences in Play Ch 8
Nuclear Family Ch 8	Extended Family Ch 8
Blended Families Ch 8	Sustenance Ch 8

Advocacy Ch 8	Permissive Parenting Ch 8
Authoritarian Parenting Ch 8	Authoritative Parenting Ch 8
Fox Parenting Inventory Ch 8	Novice Parents Ch 8
Expert Parents Ch 8	Intergenerational Transmission of Parenting Styles Ch 8

Birth Order Ch 8	Family Size Ch 8
Age Intervals Ch 8	Separation and Divorce and the Negative Effects Ch 8
Meta Analysis Ch 8	Sleeper Effects Ch 8
Parental Disengagement Ch 8	Social Competence Ch 8

Stepfamilies (Blended Families) Ch 8	Family Child Care Ch 8
Latchkey Children Ch 8	Child Care Versus Homecare Ch 8
Characteristics in a Poor Quality Child Care Program Ch 8	Characteristics in a High Quality Child Care Program Ch 8
   Ch 8	 Ch 8

Bandura: Three Separate Effects of Imitation Ch 8	Three Things Involved in the Socialization of Emotions Ch 8
Two Important Functions of Play in Animals Ch 8	Two Broad Forms of Play Ch 8
Five Different Types of Social Play Ch 8	Two Theories of Gender Roles Ch 8
Kohlberg's 3 Stages of Gender Ch 8	Three Principal Functions The Family Serves Ch 8

Six of the Most Important Features of Caregiving Ch 8	Three Distinct Groups of Children (Baumrind) Ch 8
Baumrind's Three Styles of Parenting Ch 8	Baumrind's Different Types of Parental Control Ch 8
Three Measures on Fox Parenting Inventory Ch 8	Christophereson's Seven Guidelines for Child Rearing Practices Ch 8
Three Major Caregivers Advisors Ch 8	Three Explanations Why Divorce or Separation Might Have Negative Effects Ch 8

Middle Childhood Ch 9	Fat Free Mass (Lean Body Mass) Ch 9
Fat Mass Ch 9	White Adipace Tissue Ch 9
The Growth Spurt Ch 9	Overnutrition Ch 9
Undernutrition Ch 9	Obesity Ch 9

Peak Height Velocity Ch 9	Exceptional Children Ch 9
Visually Impaired Ch 9	Mainstreaming Ch 9
Hard of Hearing Ch 9	Prelinguistic Deafness Ch 9
Postlinguistic Deafness Ch 9	Otitus Anedia Ch 9

Deaf and Dumb (Deaf Mute) Ch 9	Americal Sign Language (ASL) Ch 9
P-B, T-D, F-V Ch 9	Concrete Observation Ch 9
Conservation Ch 9	Meaning Making (Constructive Knowledge) Ch 9
Operations Ch 9	Preoperations Ch 9

Field Effects Ch 9	Rules of Logic Ch 9
Identity Ch 9	Reversibility Ch 9
Compensation Ch 9	Classes Ch 9
Series (Seriation) Ch 9	Number Ch 9

Ordinal Numbers Ch 9	Cardinal Numbers Ch 9
Information Processing Approach Ch 9	Knowledge Base Ch 9
Cognitive Strategies Ch 9	Game of Cognition Ch 9
Metacognition Ch 9	Knowing About Knowing Ch 9

Sensory Memory Ch 9	Short-Term Memory (Working Memory) Ch 9
Long-Term Memory Ch 9	Chunking Ch 9
Rehearsal Ch 9	Generative Ch 9
Scripts Ch 9	Declarative Versus Nondeclarative Memory Ch 9

Implicit Memory Ch 9	Conscious Memory Ch 9
Unconscious Memory Ch 9	General Knowledge - Semantic Memory Ch 9
Personal Memories -Episodic Memory Ch 9	Autobiographical Knowledge Ch 9
Rehearsing Ch 9	Elaborating Ch 9

Organizing Ch 9	Metacognition Ch 9
Metamemory Ch 9	Socratic Dialogue Ch 9
Cognitive Apprenticeship Ch 9	Game of Cognition Ch 9
Valid Ch 9	Reliable Ch 9

General Factor Theory	Special Abilities Theory
Ch 9	Ch 9
Fluid Abilities (Fluid Intelligence)	Crystallized Abilities (Crystallized Intelligence)
Ch 9	Ch 9
Contextual Approach (Contextual Theory of Intelligence)	Sternberg's Definition of Intelligence
Ch 9	Ch 9
Sternberg's Three Major Components of Intelligence	Metacomponents
Ch 9	Ch 9

Performance Components Ch 9	Knowledge Components Ch 9
Stanford-Binet Ch 9	Wechsler Ch 9
Individual Intelligence Tests Ch 9	Group Intelligence Tests Ch 9
"Adaptive Ability" Ch 9	Intelligence Quotient (IQ) Ch 9

WISC-III Ch 9	WAIS-R Ch 9
WPPSI Ch 9	Psychometrically Ch 9
Culture Fair IQ Tests Ch 9	Mental Retardation Ch 9
General Intellectual Functioning Ch 9	Impairment in Adaptive Behavior Ch 9

Extremely Unreliable Ch 9	AAMR American Association on Mental Retardation Ch 9
Pre-Postnatal Organic Causes of Mental Retardation Ch 9	EMR - Educable Mentally Retarded Ch 9
Moderately Retarded Ch 9	Severe Mental Retardation Ch 9
Profoundly Mentally Retarded Ch 9	Learning Disabilities Ch 9

Developmental Reading Disorder (Dyslexia or Specific Reading Disability) Ch 9	Developmental Arithmetic Disorder Ch 9
Process Disorders Ch 9	"Attention Deficit Disorder" Ch 9
Creativity Ch 9	Divergent Thinking Ch 9
Convergent Thinking Ch 9	Fluency Ch 9

Flexibility Ch 9	Originality Ch 9
Mainstreaming Ch 9	Adaptive Education Ch 9
      Ch 9	 Ch 9
     Ch 9	 Ch 9

Two Forms of Malnutrition

Ch 9

Four Factors in Obesity

Ch 9

Three Rules of Logic

Ch 9

Three Other Abilities Acquired During the Conservation Stage

Ch 9

Three Things Information-Processing Includes

Ch 9

Atkinson and Sheffrin - Three Types of Information Storage

Ch 9

Four Aspects of Processing

Ch 9

Two Limitations of Attention Span

Ch 9

Three Important Characteristics of Long-Term Memory Ch 9	Two Distinct Types of Declarative Long-Term Memory Ch 9
List 3 Basic Processes Involved in Remembering Ch 9	Paris and Lindauer: Four Sets of Circumstances Under Which Research Has Found Significant Developmental Changes Ch 9
Davies: Four Observations From Review of Studies on Children's Memories Ch 9	Four Reasons Children Do Not Play Game of Cognition Well Ch 9
Four Areas on Stanford-Binet Intelligence Test Ch 9	Four Misconceptions About IQ Ch 9

Two Features of Mental Retardation Ch 9	Two Reasons Measures at the Lower Levels of Mental Retardation are Extremely Unreliable Ch 9
Two Main Groups of Causes of Mental Retardation Ch 9	Four Categories of Mental Retardaion Ch 9
Three Types of Retardation Outlined by Special-Needs Education Ch 9	Eight Other Terms Used for Learning Disabilities Ch 9
Four Characteristics of Learning Disabilities Ch 9	Three Aspects of Student's Characteristics and Functioning Used to Determining Learning Disabilities Ch 9

Two Aspects of Intellectual Giftedness Ch 9	Heinzin - Three Approaches to Measuring Creativity Ch 9
Guilford's Factors in Creativity Ch 9	Albert and Runco - Seven Important Factors in Development of Eminence Ch 9
     Ch 9	 Ch 9

Cognition Ch 10	Metacognition Ch 10
Social Cognition Ch 10	Theory of Mind Ch 10
Empathy Ch 10	Self Referent Thought Ch 10
James' Approach to Self Worth Ch 10	Cooley's Approach to Self Worth Ch 10

Looking Glass Self Ch 10	Rosenberg Self-Esteem Scale Ch 10
Hartes Self-Perception Profile for Children Ch 10	Best Friend(s) Ch 10
Peer Group Ch 10	Sociometric Status Ch 10
Peer Rating Ch 10	Peer Nominations Ch 10

Sociogram Ch 10	Social Isolates Ch 10
Sociometric Stars Ch 10	Teacher Negatives Ch 10
Mixer Ch 10	Tuned Out Ch 10
Sociometric Rejectees Ch 10	Schooling and Measured Intelligence Ch 10

"Bloomers" Ch 10	Attribution Theory Ch 10
Internal Locus of Control Ch 10	Mastery Oriented Ch 10
External Locus of Control Ch 10	Learned Helplessness Ch 10
Characteristics of Mastery Oriented vs. Helpless Children Ch 10	Aggression Ch 10

Violence Ch 10	Imitation Ch 10
Attitude Change Ch 10	Information Processing Ch 10
Crimes Against Persons Ch 10	Physical Abuse Ch 10
Physical Neglect Ch 10	Emotional Abuse (Psychological Abuse) Ch 10

Sexual Abuse	Sexualized Behavior
Ch 10	Ch 10
Past Traumatic Stress Disorder	Characteristics of Abusive Parents
Ch 10	Ch 10
Behavior Disordered	Emotionally Disturbed
Ch 10	Ch 10
Socially Maladjusted	Resilient (Invulnerable)
Ch 10	Ch 10

Attention Defecit Hyperactivity Disorder (ADHD) Ch 10	Hyperkinesis Ch 10
Dexadrine Ch 10	Ritalin Ch 10
Paradoxical Effect Ch 10	Oppositional Defiant Disorder Ch 10
Harm Ch 10	Threat Ch 10

Challenge Ch 10	Stimulus (Demand) Overload Ch 10
Responsibility Overload Ch 10	Change Overload Ch 10
Emotional Overload Ch 10	Information Overload Ch 10
Hurried Child Ch 10	Life Change Events Ch 10

Two Approaches to Self Worth Ch 10	Five Areas in Which Children Evaluate Their Worth Ch 10
Five Findings Dealing with Investigations of Self Worth Ch 10	Two Methods of Assessing Sociometric Status Ch 10
Three Reasons Aggression Research in Children are Unrealistic Ch 10	Negative Effects of Television Ch 10
Positive Effects of Television Ch 10	Four Types of Child Maltreatment Ch 10

Three Problems in Estimating Child Sexual Abuse Ch 10	Three Difficulties in Classifying Emotional Disturbances in Children Ch 10
Diagnostic Criteria for ADHD (14) Ch 10	Two Approaches to Defining Stress Ch 10
  Ch 10	 Ch 10
  Ch 10	 Ch 10

Adolescence Ch 11	Rites of Passage Ch 11
Four Steps in Rites of Passage Ch 11	Separation Ch 11
Taboo Ch 11	Initiation Ch 11
Induction Ch 11	Discontinuous Societies Ch 11

Continuous Societies Ch 11	Formal Rites of Passage Ch 11
Strum and Drang Ch 11	Puberty Ch 11
Pubescence Ch 11	Fat-Free Mass Ch 11
Menarche Ch 11	Primary Sexual Characteristics Ch 11

Ovaries Ch 11	Testes Ch 11
Spermarche Ch 11	Age of Puberty Ch 11
Obesity Ch 11	Anorexia Nervosa Ch 11
Restrictions Ch 11	Bulimia Nervosa Ch 11

Perfectionism Ch 11	Cognitive Behavioral Therapy Ch 11
Assimilating (Piaget) Ch 11	Accommodating (Piaget) Ch 11
Equilibrating (Piaget) Ch 11	Formal Operations Ch 11
Formal vs. Concrete Thinking Ch 11	Logic of Propositions Ch 11

Information Processing Ch 11	Egocentrism Ch 11
Adolescent Egocentrism Ch 11	Imaginary Audience Ch 11
Personal Fable Ch 11	Elkind & Bowen-Imaginary Audience Scale (IAS) Ch 11
Enright & Colleagues - Adolescent Egocentrism-Sociocentrism Scale Ch 11	Morality Ch 11

Heterononmy Ch 11	Kohlberg's Stages Ch 11
Preconventional Level Ch 11	Conventional Ch 11
Postconventional Ch 11	Seventh Stage Ch 11
Positive-Negative Moral Duties Ch 11	 Ch 11

Three Important Aspects of Cognition Ch 11	Five Reasons Adolescents Underestimate the Probability for Themselves in Risk Taking Activities Ch 11
Three Things Involved in Kohlberg's "Good and Bad": Ch 11	Carroll & Rest - Four Steps in Behaving Morally Ch 11
Piaget's Two Stages of Moral Development Ch 11	Gilligan's Three Stages in Women's Moral Development Ch 11
     Ch 11	 Ch 11

Self Ch 12	Identity Ch 12
Self-Definition Ch 12	Self-Worth (Self Esteem) Ch 12
Self Image Ch 12	Offer Self-Image Questionnaire Ch 12
Offer's Facets of Self Ch 12	Psychological Self Ch 12

Social Self Ch 12	Sexual Self Ch 12
Familial Self Ch 12	Coping Self Ch 12
Sturm and Drang Ch 12	Identity vs. Role Diffusion (Erickson) Ch 12
Adolescent Moratorium Ch 12	Negative Identities Ch 12

Identity Diffusion Ch 12	Foreclosure Ch 12
Moratorium Individuals Ch 12	Emotional Distancing Ch 12
Elite Ch 12	Jocks Ch 12
Populars Ch 12	Outcasts Ch 12

Lovers-Needs Ch 12	Alienated Ch 12
Druggies Ch 12	Greaser Ch 12
Brains-Eggheads Ch 12	Normals Ch 12
Gender Roles (Sex Roles) Ch 12	Gender Ch 12

Androgynous Ch 12	Gender Typing Ch 12
Sexual Stereotypes Ch 12	Biological Differences Ch 12
Psychobiological Differences Ch 12	Verbal Ability Ch 12
Visual/Spatial Ability Ch 12	Mathematic-Science Ability Ch 12

Aggression Ch 12	Double Standard Ch 12
Attitudes Ch 12	Age of Imitation Ch 12
Masturbation Ch 12	Adolescent Pregnancy Ch 12
IUD (Intrauterine Device) Ch 12	Homosexuality Ch 12

Sexually Transmitted Diseases (STD's) (Venereal Diseases) Ch 12	Chlamydia Ch 12
Gonorrhea Ch 12	Genital Herpes Ch 12
AIDS Ch 12	Delinquency Ch 12
Gangs Ch 12	Drugs Ch 12

Drug Abuse Ch 12	Drug Dependency Ch 12
Physiological Dependency (Addiction) Ch 12	Psychological Dependency (Habituation) Ch 12
Drug Tolerance Ch 12	Dyscontrol Ch 12
Gateway Drug-Use Theory Ch 12	Marijuana (Tetrahydrocannabinol (THC) Ch 12

LSD (D-Lysergic Acid Diethylamide Tartrate) (LSD-25) Ch 12	Alcohol Ch 12
Cocaine Ch 12	Crack ("Rack") Ch 12
STP, MDA (methylamphetamines) Ch 12	PCP (Phencyclidine) Ch 12
     Ch 12	 Ch 12

Marcia's Four Types of Identity Status Ch 12	Three Stages of Socialization Ch 12
Six Different Peer Groups Ch 12	Four Areas in Which There is a Difference Between the Sexes Ch 12
Three Areas Where There Are Major Changes in Recent Decades Ch 12	Four Reasons for Adolescent Pregnancies Ch 12
List 5 STDs Ch 12	Three Reasons for the Popularity of "Crack" Ch 12

Peter Pan Syndrome Ch 13	Early Adulthood (20 to 40-45) Ch 13
Middle Adulthood (40-45 to 65-70) Ch 13	Late Adulthood (65-70 Onward) Ch 13
Youth (14-24) Ch 13	Developmental Tasks Ch 13
Self Centered Ch 13	Other Centered Ch 13

Quantitative Physical Measures Ch 13	Qualitative Physical Measures Ch 13
Stress Overload Ch 13	Type A Ch 13
Type B Ch 13	Jenkins Activity Survey Ch 13
Refractory Period Ch 13	Sexual Dysfunctions Ch 13

Erectile Dysfunctions (Impotence) Ch 13	Premature Ejaculation Ch 13
Retarded Ejaculation Ch 13	Vaginismus Ch 13
Hypoactive Sexual Desire Ch 13	Amenorrhea Ch 13
Job Ch 13	Occupation Ch 13

Career Ch 13	Vocation Ch 13
Job-Person Matching Ch 13	Developmental Models of Guidance Ch 13
Family Based Model Ch 13	Holland Vocation Preference Inventory Ch 13
Developmental Career Models Ch 13	Fantasy Period Ch 13

Tentative Period Ch 13	Realistic Period Ch 13
Exploration Ch 13	Crystallization Ch 13
Specification Ch 13	"Recycling" and a Career Ch 13
Career Self-Efficacy Expectations Ch 13	Three Reasons People Become Happier with Their Work as They Age Ch 13

Fast Trackers Ch 13	Dead Enders Ch 13
Change vs. Stability Ch 13	Riegel's Dialectical Thinking Ch 13
Dialectics Ch 13	Dialectual Stage Ch 13
Basseches' Dialectical Schemata Ch 13	Dialectual Schema Ch 13

Labouvie-Vief's Pragmatic Wisdom Ch 13	Sternberg's Contextual Theory of Intelligence Ch 13
Sternberg's Componential Theory of Intelligence Ch 13	Metacomponents Ch 13
Performance Components Ch 13	Knowledge-Acquisition Components Ch 13
Triarchic Theory of Intelligence Ch 13	Experiential Ch 13

Havighurst's Tasks of Early Adulthood Ch 13	Two Important Things in Looking at Developmental Tasks Ch 13
Coleman's Transitional Tasks Ch 13	Coleman's Three Types of Other Centered Activities Ch 13
Some Consequences of Stress Ch 13	Sources of Stress Ch 13
The Four Stages of Normal Sexual Response Ch 13	Two Important Differences Between Male and Female Sexual Responses Ch 13

Three Common Patterns of Female Sexual Response Ch 13	Two Types of Problems That Reflect Sexual Responsiveness Ch 13
Theories of Career Choice Ch 13	Scoping Styles Ch 13
Ginzberg's Three Substages Within the Realistic Period Ch 13	Super's Lifespan Career Development Ch 13
Clausen's Three Factors Related to Satisfaction Workers Experience with Their Occupations Ch 13	Three Aspects of Componential Theory Ch 13

Intimacy vs. Isolation Ch 14	Genital Ch 14
Career Consolidation Versus Self Absorption Ch 14	Developmental Level (Developmental Task) Ch 14
Rubin's Loving and Liking Scales Ch 14	Intimacy Ch 14
Passion Ch 14	Committment Ch 14

Triangular Theory of Love Ch 14	Propinquity Ch 14
Cohabitation Ch 14	Common Law Relationships Ch 14
Homosexual Lifestyle Ch 14	Never-Marrieds Ch 14
Singlehood Ch 14	"Le Gai Bachelor" Ch 14

The Separated and Divorced Ch 14	Communes Ch 14
Monogamy Ch 14	Bigamy Ch 14
Polygamy Ch 14	Polygyny Ch 14
Polgandry Ch 14	Serial Monogamy Ch 14

Adultery Ch 14	Vitalized Couples Ch 14
Devitalized Couples Ch 14	Financially Focused Couples Ch 14
Conflicted Couples Ch 14	Harmonious Marriage Ch 14
Traditional Couples Ch 14	Balanced Couples Ch 14

Marital Discord Ch 14	Dysphoria Ch 14
Marital Satisfaction Ch 14	Family Ch 14
Nuclear Families Ch 14	Extended Families Ch 14
Duvall- Life Cycle Approach Ch 14	Stage 1: To Have Children (Honeymoon Stage) Ch 14

Stages 2-5 - Childrearing Ch 14	Stage 2: Infancy Ch 14
Stage 3: Preschool Ch 14	Stage 4: Preteen School Years Ch 14
Stage 5: Teen Years Ch 14	Family Violence Ch 14
Interspousal Violence Ch 14	Sexual Assault and Aquaintance Rape Ch 14

Stranger Incidents Ch 14	Party Incidents Ch 14
Acquaintance Incidents Ch 14	Date Incidents Ch 14
Rape Shield Law Ch 14	Impulsive Self Ch 14
Imperial Self Ch 14	Interpersonal Self Ch 14

Institutional Self	Interindividual Self
Ch 14	Ch 14
Ch 14	Ch 14
Ch 14	Ch 14
Ch 14	Ch 14

Institutional Self

Interindividual Self

Erikson's Three Developmental Stages That Span Adulthood and Old Age Ch 14	Freud - Two Things Essential for a Healthy Adult Ch 14
Rubin - Three Components of Love Ch 14	Sternberg's Eight Varieties of Interpersonal Attraction Ch 14
Three Things Strongly Influencing Interpersonal Attraction Ch 14	Differences Betwee Homosexual and Heterosexual Relationships (Couples) Ch 14
Olson - Nine Major Dimensions of "Good" Marriage Ch 14	Olson - Seven Different Types of Relationships Ch 14

Six Alternative Nonexclusive Marital Lifestyles Ch 14	Two Types of Families Ch 14
Duvall's Eight Sequential Stages in the Evolution of the Family Ch 14	Three Important Developmental Tasks at the First Stage Ch 14
Three Tasks at the Preteen School Years Ch 14	Four different Types of College or University Campus Rape Ch 14
Kegan's Five Stages in the Evolution of Self Ch 14	Ch 14

Middle Adulthood Ch 15	Glaucoma Ch 15
Cataracts Ch 15	Presbycusis Ch 15
Atherosclerosis Ch 15	Arteriosclerosis Ch 15
Stroke Ch 15	Osteteoporosis Ch 15

Hormone Replacement Therapy (HRT) Ch 15	Change of Life (Climacteric) Ch 15
Menopause Ch 15	Climacteric Syndrome Ch 15
Estrogen Replacement Therapy (ERT) Ch 15	Cross Sectional Studies on Intelligence in Middle Adulthood Ch 15
Longitudinal Studies on Intelligence in Middle Adulthood Ch 15	Fluid Intelligence (Cattell) Ch 15

Crystallized Intelligence Ch 15	Experience-Intuition Ch 15
Pragmatics Ch 15	Dialectical Thinkers Ch 15
Dialectical Schemata Ch 15	Dual Careers Ch 15
Double Career (Double Track Career) Ch 15	Burnout Ch 15

Career Self-Efficacy

Ch 15

Ch 15

Ch 15

Ch 15

Ch 15

Ch 15

Ch 15

Ch 15

Signs of Menopause Ch 15	Five Reasons for Making An Involuntary Career Change Ch 15
    Ch 15	 Ch 15
    Ch 15	 Ch 15
    Ch 15	 Ch 15

Generativity Versus Self-Absorption (Erikson) Ch 16	Seasons of a Man's Life (Levinson) Ch 16
Levinson's Five Major Eros (Ages) Ch 16	Early Adulthood Ch 16
Levinson's Dream Ch 16	Age 30 Transition Ch 16
Settling Down Ch 16	Midlife Transition Ch 16

Midlife Crisis Ch 16	Purpose in Life Ch 16
"Time From Birth" vs. "Time to Death" Ch 16	Marker Events Ch 16
Middle Adulthood Ch 16	Age 50 Transition Ch 16
Seasons of a Woman's Life Ch 16	Gender Based Dreams Ch 16

Gender Splitting Ch 16	Passages (Sheehy) Ch 16
Deadline Decade Ch 16	Male-Female Differences at Midlife Ch 16
"Life Structure" Ch 16	Return of the Repressed Ch 16
Androgyny Ch 16	Freestyle fifties Ch 16

Selective Sixties Ch 16	Thoughtful Seventies Ch 16
Proud-to-be-Eighties Ch 16	Gould's Transformations Ch 16
Self Consciousness Ch 16	Midlife Crisis (Midlife Identity Crisis) Ch 16
Launching Phase (Duvall) Ch 16	Empty Nest Phase (Duvall) Ch 16

Coalition Ch 16	Stepfamilies Ch 16
Personality (Types) Ch 16	NEO Typology Ch 16
N - Neuroticism Ch 16	E - Extraversion Ch 16
O - Openness Ch 16	Satisfaction vs. Happiness Ch 16

Peck's Seven Classifications

Ch 16

Ch 16

Ch 16

Ch 16

Ch 16

Ch 16

Ch 16

Ch 16

Ageism Ch 17	"Young-Old" Ch 17
"Old-Old" Ch 17	Lifespans Ch 17
Life Expectancy Ch 17	A Genetic Theory of Aging Ch 17
Collagen Ch 17	Cell Malfunction Theories Ch 17

Cell Error Theory Ch 17	Toxin Theory of Cell Malfunction Ch 17
Free Radical Theory Ch 17	Cross Linking Theory Ch 17
Autoimmunity Ch 17	Senescence Ch 17
Primary Aging Ch 17	Osteoporosis Ch 17

Arteriosclerosis Ch 17	"Liver Spots" Ch 17
"Crow's Feet" Ch 17	Parkinson's Disease Ch 17
Acute Brain Syndrome Ch 17	Alzheimer's Disease Ch 17
Presbycusis Ch 17	Divisions of Memory Ch 17

Short Term Memory Ch 17	Long Term Memory Ch 17
Declarative Memory Ch 17	Semantic Memory Ch 17
Episodic Memory Ch 17	Nondeclarative Memory Ch 17
Digit Span Test Ch 17	Recognition Recall Ch 17

Free Recall Ch 17	Fluid Abilities Ch 17
Crystallized Abilities Ch 17	Centenarians Ch 17
Terminal Drop Ch 17	Disengagement From Life Ch 17
Mythical Thinking: Mythos Ch 17	Wisdom Ch 17

Enlightenment Ch 17	Kharma Ch 17
Mukti Ch 17	Guru Ch 17
Dialectic Ch 17	 Ch 17
    Ch 17	 Ch 17

Fisher - Five Distinct Phases of Older Adulthood Ch 17	Neugarten - Two Categories of Old Age Ch 17
In the West - Three Paths to Wisdom Ch 17	Four Dimensions of Wisdom Ch 17
Five Steps in Wise Decision Making (Dittmann Kohli and Baltes) Ch 17	Ch 17
Ch 17	Ch 17

Integrity Versus.Despair: Erikson Ch 18	Ego Differentiation Versus Work-Role Preoccupation Ch 18
Body Transcendence Versus Body Preoccupation Ch 18	Continuity With Middle Age Ch 18
Early Transition Ch 18	Revised Lifestyle Ch 18
Later Transition Ch 18	Final Period Ch 18

Life Review Ch 18	Personal Narratives Ch 18
Reminiscence Ch 18	Preretirement Ch 18
Disengagement Theory Ch 18	Activity Theory Ch 18
Surrogate-Parent Role Ch 18	Fun-Seeking-Grandparent Role Ch 18

Grandparent-As-Distant-Figure Role Ch 18	Reservoir-Of-Family-Wisdom Role Ch 18
Formal-Grandparenting Role Ch 18	Surrogate Parent Ch 18
Widows And Widowers Ch 18	Filial Responsibility (Filial Piety) Ch 18
Care Facilities For The Elderly Ch 18	Excessive Institutionalization Ch 18

Elder Abuse

Ch 18

Ch 18

Ch 18

Ch 18

Ch 18

Ch 18

Ch 18

Ch 18

Pecks' Elaboration Of Erikson (Three Stages) Ch 18	Fisher's Five Periods Of Older Adulthood Ch 18
Atchley's Seven Phases Of Retirement Ch 18	Atchley's Four Sets of Circumstances For A Positive Retirement Experience Ch 18
Five Styles of Grandparenting Ch 18	Three Personality Characteristics Leading To Happiness In Old Age Ch 18
  Ch 18	 Ch 18

Rigor Mortis Ch 19	Death Ch 19
Grief Ch 19	Mourning Ch 19
Euphemisms About Death Ch 19	Children's Understanding of Death Ch 19
Adolescent Notions of Death Ch 19	Notions of Death in Early and Middle Adulthood Ch 19

Views of Death in Late Adulthood Ch 19	Fear of Dying Ch 19
Ego Integrity Ch 19	Kubler-Ross' Five Stages of Dying Ch 19
Trajectory Ch 19	Life Trajectory Ch 19
Dying Trajectory Ch 19	Expected Swift Death Ch 19

Expected Temporary Recovery Ch 19	Expected Lingering While Dying Ch 19
Acute Crisis Phase Ch 19	Chronic Phase Ch 19
Terminal Phase Ch 19	Palliative Care Ch 19
Hospice Ch 19	Euthanasia (Mercy Killing) "Good Death" Ch 19

Active Euthanasia Ch 19	Passive Euthanasia Ch 19
Ethical Suicide Ch 19	The Living Will Ch 19
Bereavement Ch 19	Grief Ch 19
Mourning Ch 19	Short Term Effects of Bereavement Ch 19

Long Term Effects of Bereavement Ch 19	Anticipatory Grief Ch 19
Grief Work Ch 19	 Ch 19
  Ch 19	 Ch 19
  Ch 19	 Ch 19

Seven Reasons for Fearing Death Ch 19	Pattison's Three Phases of Personal Trapetories Ch 19
Two Conditions to Consider Euthanasia (In Holland) Ch 19	 Ch 19
      Ch 19	 Ch 19
      Ch 19	 Ch 19